Options
made simple

A beginner's guide to trading options for success

Options
made simple

Jacqueline Clarke
& Davin Clarke

Wrightbooks

First published in 2012 by Wrightbooks
an imprint of John Wiley & Sons Australia, Ltd
42 McDougall St, Milton Qld 4064

Office also in Melbourne

Typeset in Berkeley LT 11.5/13.4 pt

© Jacqueline Clarke 2012

The moral rights of the author have been asserted

National Library of Australia Cataloguing-in-Publication data:

Author:	Clarke, Jacqueline.
Title:	Options made simple : a beginner's guide to trading options for success / Jacqueline and Davin Clarke.
ISBN:	9780730376378 (pbk.)
Notes:	Includes index.
Subjects:	Options (Finance)
Other Authors/Contributors:	Clarke, Davin.
Dewey Number:	332.6453

Cover images and design by Peter Reardon, Pipeline Design <www.pipelinedesign.com.au>

Printed in Australia by Ligare Book Printer

10 9 8 7 6 5 4 3 2 1

Disclaimer

Contents

About the authors

Jacqueline Clarke is a private trader, chartered accountant and author of *Trading Plans Made Simple*. Together with Davin Clarke, she has over 10 years' experience in managing their private business, trading equities, options, warrants, futures and currencies. As a trader and accountant, Jacqueline has a unique understanding of risk management, trade management and how to successfully trade to produce a source of income.

Davin Clarke is principal of Tzar Corp and is a successful full-time private trader. Davin has earned his primary income from trading since 2000, and has a first-hand understanding of what it takes to trade full time. Davin provides a limited number of trading skills workshops through Tzar Corp for equities, futures and options traders. Davin is regularly sought for speaking engagements and is featured in a number of books, including *The Wiley Trading Guide*, *20 Most Common Trading Mistakes and How You Can Avoid Them* and *Real Traders, Real Money, Real Lives*.

chapter 1

What are options?

Option markets have been operating through the major stock exchanges in many countries since the 1970s. In most cases, these markets have experienced significant growth since then in both the number of options traded and the range of options available. Why? Because options are an amazing trading tool that can be used in a wide range of strategies. Option strategies can vary in time frame, risk and purpose to suit the needs of a wide range of investors and traders. In this chapter we will define what options are, how they work and some of the many ways in which they can be used to enhance your trading outcomes.

In this book, we will be referring to exchange traded options over stocks or shares, unless specified otherwise. These are options that can be bought and sold through a central exchange such as the Australian Securities Exchange (ASX), and are the most commonly traded type of option. This allows us to simplify the discussion as we introduce the various components and attributes of options.

Options also exist over exchange traded funds (ETFs), indices and currencies. There are also company issued options that have different terms and conditions from exchange traded options.

What are options?

Options are exactly as their name suggests: they provide the purchaser with an option to buy or sell an underlying financial security. Although this may sound limiting, options are amazing tools that can provide both the seller of the option and the buyer of the option with the ability to protect or hedge current stock positions, reduce their market risk, or generate additional income.

Options can be issued over a range of financial securities, including stocks, indices and foreign currency. In order to simplify the discussion, for the most part we will refer to options issued over stocks. However, the same concepts generally apply to options issued over other underlying financial securities.

An option is defined by a contract between the seller of the option and the buyer of the option. The contract gives the buyer of the option the right (or option) to buy or sell a set amount of stock at a specific price on or before a specific date. The buyer pays the seller a premium in order to acquire this right. If the buyer decides to use their option, this is referred to as 'exercising' their option. When an option buyer exercises their option, they are taking action to buy or sell the stock as specified in the option contract.

Tip

It is important to note that the buyer of an option pays a premium to have the choice to exercise their right to buy or sell a stock. They are not obligated to exercise this right. Thus, in purchasing an option they have purchased the option (not the obligation) to buy or sell the underlying stock.

The buyer of an option is referred to as the taker, as they are taking up the right to buy or sell the underlying stock.

The seller of the option is providing the buyer with the right to buy or sell the underlying stock. The seller has no control over whether the option they sold will be exercised or not. They have created an obligation to fulfil the option contract if the buyer decides to exercise the option. The seller of the option is referred to as a 'writer', as they underwrite or accept the obligation contained in the option.

Tip

The seller of an option has accepted an obligation to fulfil the option contract, if and when the buyer decides to exercise the option.

Options can be broadly divided into two categories: call options and put options.

Call options

Call options give the buyer the right (but not the obligation) to *buy* the underlying stock at a specified price on or before a specified date (expiry date). The price specified in the option contract is referred to as a strike price or exercise price. As a buyer of call options, you are hoping for the value of the underlying stock to rise. An increase in the price of the underlying stock will result in an increase in the value of your options.

The seller of call options receives a premium for taking on the obligation to sell the underlying stock to the buyer of the options at the strike price if the buyer decides to exercise the option before expiry. If the buyer exercises the option, the seller must sell the underlying stock to the buyer at the strike price. If the buyer does not exercise the option, the seller simply retains the premium and the obligation expires with the option on the expiry date. This process is illustrated in figure 1.1 (overleaf).

Figure 1.1: call option

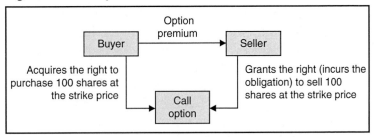

Let's run through the process of buying a call option in example 1.1.

Example 1.1

Let's say BHP has a current market price of $44 per share. You believe the market value of BHP will rise in the next few months. In order to take advantage of this expected price rise, you decide to buy a $44 call option over BHP.

This gives you the right to buy 100 shares of BHP at the strike price of $44 any time before the expiry date. If the value of BHP rises to, say, $46, your options will increase in value by $2 less a component for expired time value (we discuss this later).

You have a choice (or the option!) to either sell your option for a profit or purchase the BHP shares for $44, $2 below their current market value.

Put options

Put options give the buyer the right (but not the obligation) to *sell* the underlying stock at a specified price (strike price) on or before the expiry date. As a buyer of a put option, you are hoping the value of the underlying stock will fall as this will result in an increase in the value of your options.

The seller of a put option receives a premium for granting this right to the buyer. If the option is exercised, the option seller must buy the underlying stock at the strike price. This process is illustrated in figure 1.2.

Figure 1.2: put option

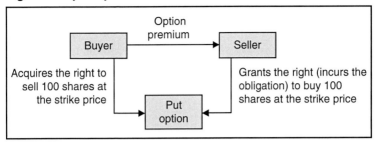

Put options are a little harder to understand, as you will make a profit if the value of the underlying stock falls. You are also buying a right to sell an asset which you may or may not own. Let's run through the purchase of a put option in example 1.2.

Example 1.2

CBA has a current market price of $52 per share. You believe the market value of CBA is too high and will fall in the next few months. You decide to buy a $52 put option over CBA.

This gives you the right to sell 100 shares of CBA at $52 any time before the expiry date. If the value of CBA falls to, say, $50, your options will increase in value by $2 less a component for expired time value (we discuss this later).

You have a choice to either sell your option for a profit or, if you own 100 CBA shares, you can sell your CBA shares for $52 per share, $2 above their current market value.

Tip

The scenarios outlined in examples 1.1 and 1.2 are shown in respect of buyers to option contracts. The scenario for the seller of the option contracts is quite different.

Option contracts

Option contracts for exchange traded options contain standard terms and conditions. Each option contract specifies the following four components for any exchange traded option:

⇨ the underlying security

⇨ the contract size

⇨ the expiry date

⇨ the exercise price (or strike price).

The option premium is not part of the standard terms of the option contract as the option premium is variable and is primarily determined by the market value of the underlying security and the time left to expiry.

Tip
It is important to understand the terms and conditions of any option before you enter into an option contract. Check the terms of the individual options to ensure they meet the objectives of your trading strategy.

Underlying security

Options traded on the ASX are only available over a limited number of company shares, referred to as the underlying securities. These underlying securities are determined by the exchange based on their own set of guidelines. The companies themselves do not have any control over the exchange traded options that are issued in relation to their shares.

Generally, you will find exchanged traded options issued over the larger companies listed on the exchange. As of April 2011, there were over 80 different companies on the ASX with exchange traded options.

Contract size

On the ASX, all exchange traded option contracts have a standard contract size of 100 as of May 2011. Prior to this date, the standard contract size for all exchange traded options contracts in Australia was 1000 shares. This brings the ASX into alignment with the US exchanges, where the standard contract size is 100 shares per option contract.

Tip

Each contract provides the buyer with the right to buy or sell 100 shares of the underlying stock. For example, if you buy five call options over BHP, this gives you the right to purchase 500 shares of BHP at the strike price any time before the option expiry date.

Expiry date

Every option has a limited life that is determined by the option expiry date. The expiry date is the last day on which the option can be traded (bought or sold) and is the date on which all unexercised options expire. For options over shares, the expiry date is usually the Thursday before the last Friday in the month.

In this book, we are only discussing American style options. American style options are options that can be exercised at any time prior to the expiry date. Most options traded on the ASX are American style options. There is, however, another style of option called European style options. European style options can only be exercised on the expiry date and not before.

As previously mentioned, the expiry date of stock options is the Thursday before the last Friday of the month. The expiry date is therefore quoted as a month, rather than a specific date. Options will be quoted as having expiry dates set on the financial quarters of March, June, September and December, plus expiry dates in each month for the next three to six months, depending upon the option category.

All exchange traded options on the ASX are categorised as either category 1 stock options or category 2 stock options. Each category of stock options has different expiry months on offer.

There are also longer term option contracts available.

Strike price

The strike price, also referred to as the exercise price, is the price at which the underlying stock can be bought or sold if the option is exercised. The ASX sets the strike prices for all options listed on the ASX options market. There are a range of strike prices set for each option expiry date for each underlying security. New strike prices will be issued as the market value of the underlying security changes. A typical range of strike prices is shown in example 1.3.

Example 1.3

The underlying shares are trading at $14.70. It is likely that options will be issued at strike prices of $11.50, $12.00, $12.50, $13.00, $13.50, $14.00, $14.50, $15.00, $15.50, $16.00, $16.50, $17.00, $17.50 and $18.00.

This provides a range of option prices to cater for the different price expectations of option traders.

Tip

The strike prices may be adjusted during the life of the option if there is a new issue of shares or a reorganisation of capital in the underlying shares. This is because a new issue or capital reorganisation (such as a share split) will affect the price of the underlying shares.

Premium

The option premium is the only component that is not standardised by the exchange. The premium is the price at which the option is bought and sold between a buyer and seller.

The price at which shares are bought and sold on the stock exchange is determined by the forces of supply and demand. Buyers put in bids to buy the stock, sellers put in offers to sell their stock, and where they meet determines the market price. This is not the case for options.

Option premiums are determined by a combination of factors, including the market value of the underlying security, the strike price of the option and the time to expiry. We will discuss pricing of options in chapter 4.

Option premiums (or prices) over stocks are quoted as 'cents per share'. To calculate the total premium for a particular option, you need to multiply the 'cents per share' by the number of shares covered by the option (usually 100). Thus, an option quoted on the exchange at $1.50 would cost you $150.00 to buy ($1.50 per share by 100 shares per contract). Of course, you would also have your transaction fees on top of this, being your brokerage and exchange fees.

Listing of option prices

Exchange traded options are listed on the stock exchange in the same way as other listed securities. The options are shown as a five or six letter code. The first three letters of the code are the same as the code for the underlying stock. The fourth and fifth letters are used to indicate the expiry month and option series. Occasionally, the options will have six letters if required.

For example, Woolworths Limited is listed on the ASX as the code WOW. Options that have Woolworths Limited as the underlying stock would have codes such as WOWXA.

Options versus shares

Investors in the stock market are buying a number of shares in a particular company. This is a tangible asset. The shares they have bought represent a part ownership in the company, which is represented by the net assets that the company holds. When you buy shares in a company, you are in control of your investment. You can decide how long you wish to hold those shares and when you wish to sell them, and you can specify the price at which you wish to sell them (although there is no guarantee that a buyer will pay the price you ask). You also receive the right to receive dividends from your shares and most shares give the owner the right to vote at shareholder meetings.

Options, on the other hand, are an intangible asset. They are not represented by any physical underlying assets. The owner of an option does not hold an equity position in the underlying stock. The option is simply a contractual right to take action. As a result, the value of an option is only a fraction of the price of the underlying stock.

As a buyer of options, you also face a limited time period in which your right exists. Remember we defined an option as a contract that gives the buyer of the option the right (or option) to buy or sell a set amount of stock at a specific price on or before a specific date (the expiry date). So your option ceases to exist at the end of trading on the expiry date (or the date on which you exercise the option). So the buyer of the option has bought an asset that has a limited life. If not exercised or sold before the expiry date, the option will cease to exist and expire worthless.

Option buyers also face another limitation. The option contract specifies the price at which the option can be exercised. Unlike stocks, where you can decide at what price you wish to sell, options do not have such flexibility. The option contract specifies the price at which you can exercise the option (the strike price) and therefore the price at which you can buy or sell the underlying stock is preset.

We will introduce the concept of pricing here just to illustrate how an intangible asset can hold value—and, in particular, how an intangible asset that will be worthless at expiry can hold value! We will talk about option pricing in more detail in chapter 4.

Option pricing

The premium price (or value) of an option is determined primarily by two factors: intrinsic value and time value. Intrinsic value is determined by the difference in the market price of the underlying stock and the price at which the option can be exercised (the strike price).

If you own an option to buy a stock at $20 and the current market price of the stock is $22, then you would expect that your option would be worth $2. The intrinsic value of the option arises because the option gives you the right to buy the stock at $2 less than the current market value of the stock.

The second component of the option price is time value. This is the value that is given to the possibility that the market will move in your favour during the life of the option and you will generate a profit on your option. Time value is primarily determined by the amount of time left on the option until it expires. As such, time value will decrease the closer we get to the expiry date. At expiry, the time value will be zero. So, in essence, the value of an option is determined by the difference in the strike price and the market price of the underlying stock, plus a value that represents the possibility of the market moving in your favour before the expiry date of the option.

Option sellers

Another significant difference between shares and options is in relation to the seller, or writer of the option. When selling shares, once the seller settles on the transaction he or she has no further obligations or rights in relation to those shares. A seller of an option contract, however, takes on a significant obligation. They have collected a premium in return for underwriting the obligation to fulfil the option contract. If the buyer of a call option decides to exercise the option, the seller must sell the underlying shares to the option holder at the strike price. If the buyer of a put option decides to exercise the option, the seller must buy the underlying shares from the option holder at the strike price.

Comparing stocks and options

In table 1.1 we do a quick comparison of some of the attributes of stock ownership compared with options as discussed in this section.

Table 1.1: comparing stocks and options

	Stocks	Options
Type of asset	*Tangibile asset*	*Intangibile asset*
	Represents partial ownership of a company	Represents a right to buy or sell an underlying stock
Period of ownership	*Unlimited*	*Limited*
	The buyer can decide how long they wish to hold their shares (subject to company restructures or insolvency).	The option ceases to exist on the expiry date.
Market price	*Determined by the market forces (buyers and sellers)*	*Determined by the intrinsic value of the option plus a value for the time left to expiry*
	The stock owner can sell their shares at any price at which they can find a willing buyer. Similarly, a buyer can purchase shares at any price at which they can find a willing seller.	For call options, the intrinsic value is the difference between the market value of the underlying stock and the strike price, if the market price is above the strike price.
	Current market price is quoted on the stock exchange and subject to change.	For put options, the intrinsic value is the difference between the market value of the underlying stock and the strike price, if the market price is below the strike price.
		The time value will decrease as we approach the expiry date, at which time the time value will be zero.

	Stocks	Options
Strike price	Not applicable	*Specified in the contract* This is the price at which the buyer of the option can exercise their right to buy (call option) or sell (put option) the underlying security.
Seller	No further obligation or benefits after the sale	Sellers of options receive a premium and retain an obligation to fulfil the option contract if it is exercised.

So there are some marked differences in owning shares to owning options. Some of these taken in isolation may appear to highlight the negatives of trading options. However, many of these attributes can become assets and advantages depending on your strategy, the type of option used and whether you are the seller or the buyer.

In chapter 2, we will explore some of the advantages of trading options and why you might consider trading options as part of your overall trading strategy. We will also outline some of the risks that you need to consider before buying or selling options.

Chapter summary

⇨ Options provide the buyer of an option with the right, but not the obligation, to buy or sell an underlying security.

⇨ Options can be issued over a large range of securities, including stocks, indices and currencies.

⇨ Options are defined by the contract, which specifies the underlying security, the strike price, the expiry date and the contract size.

⇨ The buyer pays the seller a premium for the option.

⇨ The seller of an option has granted the buyer the right to buy or sell the underlying security. They therefore have an obligation to fulfil the terms of the option if the buyer chooses to exercise the option.

⇨ Options are divided into two main types: call options and put options.

⇨ Call options grant the buyer the right to buy the underlying security at the strike price at any time up to the expiry date.

⇨ Put options grant the buyer the right to sell the underlying security at the strike price at any time up to the expiry date.

⇨ Exchange traded options have standardised terms that cover the underlying security, the contract size, the expiry date and the strike price.

⇨ Options are an intangible asset, as an option is a right and does not represent ownership of any physical underlying assets.

⇨ Options have a limited life span and cease to exist at expiry.

⇨ Options are very flexible and versatile trading instruments that can be used in a variety of trading strategies.

⇨ Some option strategies can involve a high level of risk, while other option strategies reduce your investment risk.

chapter 2

Advantages and risks

In this chapter, we will outline some of the main advantages of trading in options and why you might consider buying or selling options as a part of your overall trading strategy. We will also consider the major risks in buying and selling options, taking note that the risks involved in options are significantly different for buyers of options compared with the risks for sellers of options.

Advantages of option trading

When buying an option, you are investing in an asset with no tangible value, with a limited life, and which may be worthless within a few months. Taken in isolation, these attributes may lead you to believe that trading options is a futile endeavour. However, as you will soon discover, there are many advantages of trading options that can be used in a wide range of strategies. And as you learn more, you will see that they are very flexible tools that can be used to create income, protect profits and reduce risk, to name a few examples.

Options are considered by many to be a high risk investment. This may be in part due to a lack of understanding about options generally and how they can be used. In fact, options can be effectively used to *reduce* risk. The strategies you can employ with options range from high risk to very conservative.

We will now outline some of the main advantages of options. These are broad attributes that apply to options. As we discuss the types of options in more detail and the strategies that can be applied to each type of option, you will clearly see the advantages (and disadvantages) of trading options.

It is also interesting to note that an advantage to a seller will often translate as a disadvantage to the buyer and vice versa. The reason this works in the market is that the reason or strategy employed by the seller is often quite different from the reason that the buyer has entered into the contract.

Tip

When evaluating the advantages of using options, you also need to consider the risks associated with your particular option strategy.

The advantages we will discuss are:

⇨ risk management

⇨ speculation

⇨ leverage

⇨ diversification

⇨ income generation.

Risk management

Options provide investors with the ability to manage risk within their portfolio. Options can provide an investor with a hedge against falls in the price of their current stock holdings. It can effectively allow an investor to lock in some profits on their holding, without having to physically sell their shares.

This can be advantageous when an investor wishes to retain their shares for a longer term or does not wish to realise a capital gain by selling their investment at the current time.

For instance, buying a put option allows you to purchase the right to sell your current shares at an advantageous price, if you are expecting a fall in the price of those shares before the expiry date of the option. This will allow an investor to make a gain on the put options that will offset a loss on the physical shares, in the event that the shares do in fact fall in value. Let's consider this in example 2.1.

Example 2.1

You own 3000 shares in a stock currently trading at $10.50. You would like to lock in some profit at this price as you feel that the price is likely to fall in the short term.

To effect this strategy, you buy 30 put option contracts with a strike price of $10.50. This purchase costs you $0.20 per share contained in each contract (with 100 shares in each contract).

This purchase gives you the right to sell 3000 shares at $10.50 any time before the option expiry date.

If the stock price subsequently falls, your put option will increase in value by a similar amount (less any expired time value). Thus you are protecting yourself against a fall in the price of your stock. Any fall in the value of your stock will be offset by a rise in the value of your options.

If the stock price remains at or above $10.50, then you would either not exercise your option or sell your option close to the expiry date (although it would be worth very little).

If the stock price does fall to, say, $9.50, then the value of your put options would increase by $1.00 (less any expired time value). You could then sell these options for approximately $1.00 and realise a profit of $3000.00. This will offset the fall in value of your share holding of a similar amount.

In effect, you have paid $600.00 for your options to provide you with protection against a fall in the price of your stock position.

Speculation

The ability to trade over the internet and the listing of options on the ASX make it very easy to buy and sell options. The ease of trading options makes it possible for traders to buy an option contract with the intention of selling the option before the expiry date for a profit. The trader will have an expectation of an increase in the price of the option (due to a change in price of the underlying security) and no intention of ever exercising the option.

If your option has intrinsic value, the value of your option will change very much in line with the change in value of the underlying stock. You will also see a fall in value that is unrelated to any change in value of the underlying security but is due to a fall in the time value of the option as it nears expiry. Example 2.2 illustrates how option values move with changes in the value of the underlying stock. These movements are for options that have intrinsic value in their premium.

Example 2.2

As a speculator, you can purchase call options if you are expecting the price of the underlying security to rise. As the price of the underlying security rises, the intrinsic value of your options will increase by a similar amount.

If you are expecting the price of the underlying security to fall, your strategy might be to buy put options. As the price of the underlying security falls, the intrinsic value of your options will increase by a similar amount.

In order to generate a profit, you need the value of the underlying security to move in your favour before the expiry date and you would need to sell your option on or before the expiry date.

When buying and then selling American style stock options as a strategy to generate a short-term profit, you need to ensure you sell your options before the expiry date. This requires the price of the underlying stock to move in your favour prior to the expiry date.

Leverage

Leverage is the ability to generate the same level of return from a potential investment, but using a smaller initial outlay. Purchasing a call option with intrinsic value exposes you to a similar gain or loss that you would achieve if you owned the actual shares. However, the options only cost you a fraction of the price of the underlying stock. This allows you to benefit from a change in the price of a stock without having to pay the full price of the stock.

Leverage does come with additional risk. Although the gains are magnified through the use of leverage, so too are any losses. Example 2.3 illustrates how leverage can generate a higher percentage return than can direct investment.

Example 2.3

	Option	Stock
Purchase price per share	$0.35	$4.00
Number of shares/options	30	3000
Purchase cost	$1 050.00	$12 000.00
Stock price on sale		$4.40
Option price on sale*	$0.72	
Sale proceeds	$2 160.00	$13 200.00
Net profit**	$1 110.00	$1 200.00
Percentage return	105%	10%

* The option price is calculated as $0.35 initial value, plus the $0.40 increase in the underlying stock price, less $0.03 to represent the loss in time value between the purchase date and sale date of the option.

** The above example does not take into account any transaction costs.

As you can see from example 2.3, your percentage returns can be magnified as a result of the leverage achieved through the use of options. It is important to note that your losses can be equally magnified in some instances. However, when purchasing an option your loss will always be limited to the premium you paid for the option.

> *Tip*
>
> *When speculating using options, you need to account for the fall in time value of your option and your transaction costs when assessing your trading opportunity.*

Diversification

The use of options can provide you with the opportunity to benefit from the movement in the price of a stock at a fraction of the stock price. This allows you to build a diversified portfolio for a lower initial outlay. This does come at a cost as your options include a value for the time to expiry, which will reduce to zero over the life of the option.

Income generation

When writing (selling) an option, you receive an upfront premium from the buyer of your option. You keep this premium, whether or not the option is exercised. This premium can create an income stream if carefully selected options are sold on a systematic basis. If the options are not exercised, the seller retains the premium and has no further obligation.

There are several strategies based around selling options to generate premium income. The aim is to sell options that are unlikely to be exercised, or buy back (close out) your options prior to the expiry date if there is a risk they will be exercised.

Risks of option trading

Although there are numerous advantages to options, like all financial investments there are also risks associated with trading in options. The risks vary depending upon the type of option and are quite different for the buyer and the seller.

As with any financial investment, you should only trade options if you understand how they work and how they fit with your overall trading or investment strategy. In addition, there are a number of risks that are specific to options that you should be aware of and prepared to manage.

The risks we will discuss are:

⇨ market risk

⇨ risk of expiring worthless

⇨ risk due to leverage

⇨ potential for unlimited losses (as a seller of options)

⇨ risk of margin calls (as a seller of options)

⇨ liquidity risk.

Market risk

For an option buyer, market risk is the risk that the market value of your options will decrease, thus not moving in line with your expectation or speculation. The market value of your options is primarily affected by the market value of the underlying security, but is also affected by the time to expiry, volatility of the price of the underlying security and even movements in interest rates.

Market risk for the option writer is the risk that the market value of the underlying shares will move to create or increase the intrinsic value of the option. This will increase the chance of the option being exercised or create a loss for the seller in closing their position.

You need to ensure you have a plan to manage your market risk and have a strategy if the value of your options does not move in your direction. Option pricing is discussed in more detail in chapter 4.

Risk of expiring worthless

Every option has an expiry date and therefore has a limited life. The expiry date is the day on which you must either sell the option or exercise the option, or the option will expire worthless. If an option has no intrinsic value, the value of the option will decrease as you approach the expiry date and your time value erodes (this is referred to as time decay). On expiry, the time value will be zero. If there is no intrinsic value in your option, it will expire worthless.

Intrinsic value will only be present in an option in the following circumstances:

⇨ For call options, intrinsic value will be inherent when the market value of the underlying stock is higher than the strike price of the option. The intrinsic value will then be equal to the difference in these two amounts. This arises because you have the option to buy the underlying stock at a price below the current market value.

⇨ For put options, the situation is the reverse. Your option will have intrinsic value when the market value of the underlying stock is below the strike price of the option. The intrinsic value will then be equal to the difference in these two amounts. This is because you can sell the underlying security for a price above the current market value.

The risk of an option expiring worthless is a risk that the buyer of an option has to bear. This is in fact an advantage for the seller, as they profit from the option premium they collect when an option expires worthless.

Risk due to leverage

Just as leverage has the potential to magnify your profits on a trade, leverage equally has the potential to magnify your losses. A relatively small change in the value of the underlying security can result in a large percentage change in the value of the option. When buying an option, the option price is only a fraction of the price of the underlying stock; however, your profit or loss on the option is close to the amount you would make if you had traded the underlying stock at its full value.

Tip

Even though leverage has the potential to magnify your profit or loss on an option contract, when buying options your loss is always limited to the premium you paid for the option.

Potential for unlimited losses (as a seller of options)

Sellers of options take on an obligation to sell (call options) or buy (put options) the underlying stock at the strike price if the option is exercised by the buyer of the option. If you have sold call options, you have the obligation to sell the underlying stock at the strike price if your option is exercised by the buyer. If you already own the stock, you are losing the value between the current market price of the stock and the strike price. If you do not own the underlying stock, you have sold an uncovered option. You will have to buy the stock on the market at the current market value and deliver it to the option buyer who has exercised the option. As the market value of the underlying stock has no theoretical limit, your losses on selling uncovered call options are potentially unlimited.

As a seller of put options, you have the obligation to buy the underlying stock at the strike price if your option is exercised by the buyer. If the market value of the underlying stock fell to or near zero you are still obligated to buy the stock, which is near worthless, at the strike price. As the underlying stock price can only fall to zero, your losses as a seller of put options are only limited to the value of the underlying stock at the strike price.

Risk of margin calls (as a seller of options)

When you sell an option, you are required to provide security (referred to as a margin) to show that you are able to meet your obligations if the option is exercised. This margin can be in the form of the underlying security (if a call option), cash or other collateral. If the value of the option increases, thus going against you as a seller, you may be required to provide additional margin to cover the increase in your obligation.

Generally, margins are required to be paid within 24 hours, but this time frame is set by your broker. If you fail to provide additional margin upon request within the required time frame, your broker will be able to close out your option position or liquidate some or all of your current share holdings to meet your margin requirements.

Liquidity risk

Liquidity risk is the risk that you will be unable to close or exit your option position at a fair price when you wish to do so. Market makers are the firms that provide bid prices (price you receive on selling an option) and offer prices (price you pay on buying an option) for a range of options. They will provide a market for options for the most part; however, they do have scope in terms of the prices, number of options and times that they must quote a bid and ask price for an option. Thus, you may not be able to close your position if market conditions, such as high volatility, have allowed the market makers to significantly increase the spread (distance between the bid price and the offer price) on the option prices quoted, withdraw their bid and offer for a time period, or reduce the number of option contracts they include in their offer and bid quotes.

Tip

In times of high volatility, the price of your options may not move as you expect. It is possible that the value of the underlying security may move in your direction; however, the option value may be adjusted for the risk of significant movement in the underlying security (the high volatility), meaning that your option position does not reflect any profit on the transaction.

Chapter summary

⇨ It is important to understand both the advantages and risks involved in trading options before you decide to include options as part of your trading or investment strategy.

⇨ A risk for a buyer of an option can often translate into an advantage for the seller of the option.

⇨ The main advantages from trading options are:

  ¤ risk management

  ¤ speculation

  ¤ leverage

  ¤ diversification

  ¤ income generation.

⇨ Options can provide an investor with the ability to manage risks on their current portfolio by creating a hedge against a potential adverse movement in the market price of their current share holdings.

⇨ Options provide another financial instrument that can be used by traders to generate short-term profits on the stock market.

⇨ Options can provide the buyer with the advantage of leverage. This gives them exposure to a similar profit or loss if they had invested in the underlying stock at its full value, for only a fraction of the market price of the underlying stock.

⇨ As options cost only a fraction of the price of the underlying security, you can gain exposure to a large range of stocks with a relatively small outlay compared with investing in those stocks directly.

⇨ Premiums from selling options can provide a means of income generation for a savvy option trader.

⇨ The main risks involved in trading options are:

  ⊭ market risk

  ⊭ risk of expiring worthless

  ⊭ risk due to leverage

  ⊭ potential for unlimited losses

  ⊭ risk of margin calls

  ⊭ liquidity risk.

⇨ Like all financial investments, there is the risk that the market price will move in a direction that results in a loss.

⇨ All options have a limited life determined by the expiry date. As a buyer of options, if the market price of the underlying security does not move sufficiently in your direction before the expiry date, your option may expire worthless.

⇨ Leverage can magnify your losses as well as your profits.

⇨ As a seller of uncovered call options, you are exposed to the potential of unlimited losses.

⇨ As a seller of put options, you are exposed to losses equal to the value of the underlying security at the strike price of the option.

⇨ As a seller of options, you are required to provide a margin and may be exposed to margin calls that need to be met within a short time frame (often 24 hours).

⇨ Lack of liquidity in the options markets, particularly in times of high price volatility, may make it difficult to close or exit an option position.

chapter 3

Types of options

In this chapter we will explore in more detail the various types of options that are available and how they work. We have included two summary tables at the start of this chapter for you to refer to as you read through the detail, which will give you an overall picture of how the options work.

Towards the end of the chapter we will introduce some different types of options that are available, including company issued options and index options and how they vary from exchange traded stock options.

Summary of call options and put options

The two main types of options are call options and put options. A call option is the right to buy 100 shares of an underlying stock and a put option is the right to sell 100 shares of an underlying stock. Before we go into the detail of call and put options, in tables 3.1 and 3.2 (overleaf) we have provided a summary of the main aspects of these options.

Table 3.1: call options

	Buyer/taker	Seller/writer
Definition	Acquires right to buy: 100 shares of the underlying stock at the strike price on or before the expiry date	Has the obligation to sell: 100 shares of the underlying stock at the strike price if exercised before the expiry date
Premium	Pays a premium to the seller	Receives a premium
Market value of stock increases	Intrinsic value of the option increases as the market value of the underlying stock increases, if the market value of the underlying stock is higher than the strike price. The buyer will generate a profit if the underlying stock value increases by enough to cover the premium paid and any fall in time value of the option.	
Market value of stock decreases	Intrinsic value of the option decreases as the market value of the underlying stock decreases. If the market value of the underlying stock is below the strike price, exercising your option would result in buying the underlying stock at a price higher than the current market value. Thus, the option has no intrinsic value and changes in the option price will represent a fall in time value only.	
Profit potential	Profit is unlimited. Profit is determined by the increase in the market value of the underlying stock, less the premium paid and loss of time value.	Profit is limited to the premium received.
Risk of loss	Losses are limited to the premium paid.	Losses are potentially unlimited but only occur if the option is sold at a loss or exercised against the seller.
Speculating	Speculating that the market value of the underlying stock will increase.	Speculating that the market value of the underlying stock will remain stable or fall.

Table 3.2: put options

	Buyer/taker	Seller/writer
Definition	Acquires right to sell: 100 shares of the underlying stock at the exercise price on or before the expiry date	Has the obligation to buy: 100 shares of the underlying stock at the exercise price if exercised before the expiry date
Premium	Pays a premium to the seller	Receives a premium
Market value of stock increases	Intrinsic value of the option decreases as the market value of the underlying stock increases. If the market value of the underlying stock is above the strike price, exercising your option would result in selling the underlying stock at a price lower than the current market value. Thus the option has no intrinsic value and changes in the option price will represent a fall in time value only.	
Market value of stock decreases	Intrinsic value of the option increases as the market value of the underlying security decreases if the market value of the underlying stock is lower than the strike price. The buyer will generate a profit if the underlying stock value decreases by enough to cover the premium paid and any fall in time value of the option.	
Profit potential	Profit is limited to the value of the underlying stock at the strike price less the premium paid. Profit is determined by the decrease in market value of the underlying stock.	Profit is limited to the premium received.
Risk of loss	Losses limited to the premium paid.	Losses limited to the value of the underlying stock at the strike price less the premium received.
Speculating	Speculating that the market value of the underlying stock will decrease.	Speculating that the market value of the underlying stock will remain stable or increase.

Option buyers (takers)

An investor or trader who is buying options is generally anticipating a significant movement in the price of the underlying security before the expiry date of the option. Options provide the buyer with the opportunity to profit from this expected price movement, without having to provide capital to cover the full cost of the underlying security. However, this leverage does come with a cost inherent in the time value of the options.

Options also provide option buyers with limited risk. Their maximum loss on any option trade will be the amount they pay for the option (plus transaction costs). For example, let's assume you purchase a call option on CBA for $1, and over the next few weeks the price of CBA falls by $2. If you had purchased the CBA shares, you would have lost $2 per share. However, by purchasing the options, your loss is always limited to the option premium you paid, which in this case is $1 per share.

Tip

The buyer of an option pays a premium in order to acquire the right to buy or sell the underlying securities. This premium represents both the cost of this right and the maximum possible loss on this transaction. Regardless of the movement in the market value of the underlying security, the option buyer's maximum loss on taking an option is the premium they paid for the option.

It is important to remember that option buyers have the right but not the obligation to exercise their options. If the option holder does not wish to actually exercise the option and effect a transfer to the underlying stock, they can close out their position (effectively sell their options).

According to the ASX, as at November 2010 on average only 15 per cent of all options traded on the exchange are exercised. Of the remaining 85 per cent, 60 per cent of these are closed out and 25 per cent expire worthless. So a significant number of options are bought and sold by investors and traders for purposes other than acquiring the underlying stock.

Option sellers (writers)

Option writers charge a premium for selling options. Many options writers sell options with the intention of generating an income from the option premiums. As a result, these option writers are generally expecting that the price of the underlying security will remain flat or steady. This will result in the option losing value as the time value of the option decreases.

Option writers may also be looking to generate larger profits from the movement in the underlying security. The writer of call options will be speculating on a fall in the price of the underlying security and the writer of put options will be speculating on an increase in the price of the underlying security.

As the decision to exercise an option rests with the buyer, option writers can have their options exercised at any time before expiry. They will not know if or when their options may be exercised. However, they are more likely to be exercised when the option is 'in-the-money' and close to expiry. An option is in-the-money when it contains intrinsic value. That is, for a call option, the market value is above the strike price of the option and for a put option the market value is below the strike price of the option.

Option writers also carry a much higher level of risk compared with option buyers. Whereas the total risk for the option buyer is limited to the option premium, the situation is quite different for option writers. A writer of uncovered call options is theoretically exposed to unlimited risk as they are exposed to increases in the value of the underlying stock. As the market value of the underlying stock increases, the option writer has the risk of having to purchase the underlying stock at its market value, however high that might be.

A writer of put options is exposed to the value of the underlying stock at the strike price. The option writer has the obligation to buy this stock from the option holder if it is exercised at the strike price. If the market value of the stock falls to zero and the option is exercised, the option holder is required to buy the worthless stock from the option holder at the strike price.

Call options

A call option is the right to buy 100 shares of the underlying stock at the strike price. This right can be exercised by the taker (buyer) of the option at any time from when they purchase the option until the expiry date of the option.

Buyers of call options

By investing in a call option you will generate a profit on your option if the market value of the underlying stock rises by enough to cover the premium you paid for the call option and any reduction in time value that occurs while you hold the option. This increase in market value must occur *before* the expiry date of your option. The buyer of a call option faces a time deadline in which to generate a profit from the transaction. If you decided to invest in the underlying stock directly, you can wait for your predicted increase in market value in order to realise a profit on your investment. However, by investing in a call option over the same stock, you do not have this benefit. You will fail to generate a profit on your call option if the market value of the underlying stock does not increase by a sufficient amount before the expiry date of the call option.

Tip

Time is a key factor in determining if an option buyer generates a profit from their call option. The market value of the underlying stock must increase by a sufficient amount before the expiry date for the buyer of a call option to realise a profit on their investment.

The buyer of a call option is speculating (and hoping!) that the market value of the underlying stock will increase in value before the expiry date of the option. If the market value of the underlying stock increases, and the strike price is less than the market value of the underlying stock, the value of the option will also increase. This means that the buyer of the call option can either sell the call at a profit, or acquire the stock at a price below the current market value.

Sellers of call options

The seller of a call option is hoping that the market value of the underlying stock will fall, or remain flat, as this will result in a decrease in value of the call option. The seller can then buy back the option at a lower price and realise a profit. Alternatively, if the value of the underlying stock is below the strike price of the option, it is highly unlikely that the option will be exercised. The buyer of the call option is not going to buy stock at a price higher than the current market price! In this event, the seller will simply wait until the expiry date, at which time the option will expire worthless. In this example, the seller would retain the premium they received on the initial sale of the option as a profit.

Understanding call options from a seller's perspective is a little more difficult to begin with. As a buyer of a call option, you are following a buy-hold-sell pattern, which is much the same as investing in the stock directly. The main differences are that you are able to expose yourself to the stock at a fraction of the price of the actual stock and you have a limited time period in which to sell or exercise your option.

When selling a call option, you are reversing this pattern and following a sequence of sell-hold-buy, or just sell-hold. You are selling your option first, hoping for the price of your option to fall and then buying it back at a lower price.

Or even better still, you sell-hold and if the option has no intrinsic value at expiry, you have no need to buy back at all. This process is illustrated in figure 3.1.

Figure 3.1: time patterns for option buyers and sellers

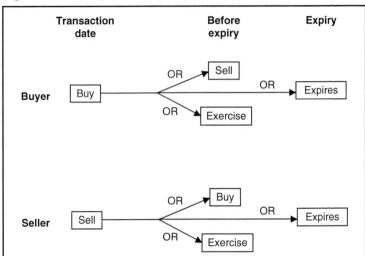

Put options

A put option gives the option buyer the right to sell 100 shares of the underlying stock at the strike price. This right can be exercised by the taker (buyer) of the option at any time from when they purchase the option until the expiry date of the option.

Buyers of put options

The value of a put option will increase as the market value of the underlying security decreases below the strike price of the option. This is because the option holder has the right to sell their stock at a set price, even though the market value of the stock is falling. By buying a put option you will generate a profit on your option if the market value of the underlying stock falls by enough to cover the premium you paid for the put option. However, as with all options, this fall in market value must occur *before* the expiry date of your option.

Put options provide the option buyer with an opportunity to speculate on falls in the market value of a stock. Speculating on falls in stock prices directly in the stock market is referred to as trading short or short selling. Short selling of stocks directly can be difficult and expensive. As such, put options can provide an effective means for trading short. However, once again time is a factor to consider when trading or investing in options. In order to generate a profit on your put option, the market value of the underlying stock must decrease by a sufficient amount before the expiry date of the put option.

Tip

Put options can be useful to protect profits on your existing stock holdings. The premium can be considered to be like paying for insurance against losses due to a fall in the market value of your shares.

The buyer of a put option is speculating that the market value of the underlying stock will decrease in value before the expiry date of the option. If the market value of the underlying stock decreases, the value of the option will increase (if the option is in-the-money). This means that the buyer of the put option can either sell the put option at a profit or, if they hold the underlying security, sell this stock at a price above the current market value.

Instead of purely speculating, the buyer of a put option may also be taking the option position to protect profits on existing share holdings. For example, if they hold shares that have experienced a recent increase in price and they believe that the stock value will fall in the short term, rather than selling their stock they could buy a put option that would protect their profit. If the market value of the underlying stock did fall, the fall in value of their stock holding would be offset in part by the gain on their put options.

Sellers of put options

The seller of a put option is hoping that the market value of the underlying stock will rise, or remain flat, as this will result in a decrease in value of the put option. The seller can then buy back the option at a lower price and realise a profit. Alternatively, if the value of the underlying stock is above the strike price of the option, it is highly unlikely that the option will be exercised. The buyer of the put option is not going to sell their stock at a price lower than the current market price! In this event, the seller will simply wait until the expiry date, at which time the option will expire worthless. The seller would retain the premium they received on the initial sale of the option as a profit.

When selling a put option, just as selling a call option, you are following a sequence of sell-hold-buy, or just sell-hold. You are selling your option first, hoping for the price of the option to fall and then buying it back at a lower price. Or, even better still, you sell-hold and if the market value of the underlying security is above the strike price, the option has no intrinsic value and you have no need to buy back at all.

Let's have a look at these price movements for in-the-money options in figure 3.2.

Figure 3.2: price movement for in-the-money options

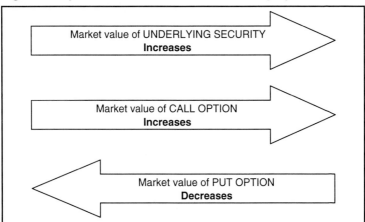

Company issued options

Company issued options are options that are issued directly by a company. The company sets the terms and conditions of the options and they are not listed on an exchange. Generally, these options are issued to current shareholders or key personnel for the purposes of raising additional capital. These options give the shareholders the right to purchase new shares at a set price (exercise price) before a set date. In this instance, the company is the writer of the options and has the obligation to fulfil any options that are exercised.

As these options are issued by the individual companies for specific purposes, the terms and conditions of these options are determined by the company issuing the options. Therefore, the terms and conditions, including expiry date, exercise price and number of shares covered per option, will vary. If you are issued these types of options, you need to read the documentation carefully to determine the terms and conditions and the procedures required to exercise the option.

Index options

Index options are options over a share price index. A share price index is a group of listed shares. Each share in the index is given a weighting and a calculation is done using their weighting and current market price to determine the index value. This index value is expressed in points.

Consequently, index options give you exposure to a group of securities that comprise the sharemarket index. This allows you to trade a position on the market as a whole, or the market sector or companies that make up the index you wish to trade.

In Australia, the ASX has options over the S&P/ASX 200 index. This is an index that is calculated based on the top 200 companies listed on the ASX. Trading these options effectively exposes you to movements in the overall Australian stock market.

The value of your index options will vary with movements in the value of the index, which is reflective of the overall value of the group of securities it represents. Movements in the S&P/ASX 200 index are seen as reflective of the movement in the overall sharemarket, as this index covers the largest 200 stocks listed on the ASX.

There are a few differences to note between index options and stock options, which we will now discuss.

⇨ *Index options are European style options.* This means that index options cannot be exercised prior to the settlement date. You can, however, buy and sell them prior to the exercise date. Being European style options also means that there is no risk of early exercise for the seller. The sellers of index options do not need to worry about their options being exercised before the expiry date.

⇨ *Index options are cash settled.* This means that the value of the index option is calculated on settlement date, and upon exercise all options are closed out with the relevant cash value. If your index option contract is worth something, you will be paid the value. If your index option has no value on expiry date, it simply expires worthless. The cash amount you receive on expiry is the difference between the settlement value of the index and the exercise value of the index. You will only receive a cash value if your index option is in-the-money.

⇨ *Settlement value on expiry is calculated using opening prices.* The settlement amount is calculated using the opening price of each stock in the underlying index on the morning of the expiry date. For each stock in the index, the first traded price, or opening price, is recorded for each stock in the index. The value of the index is then calculated using these opening values.

⇨ *The premium and strike price of index options are expressed in points.* The index itself is expressed in points, so it follows that the premium and strike price of an index option are also expressed in points. Each index has an index multiplier, which converts these points to a dollar value. For example, an index option with an index multiplier of $25 and quoted at a premium of 20 points would cost you $500 to buy (20 points × the index multiplier of $25 = $500). Similarly, the value of an index option contract is calculated as the strike price of the option multiplied by the index multiplier.

Benefits of index options

There are a number of key benefits of investing in index options. The same benefits of investing in share options that we discussed in chapter 1 also apply to index options. They are risk management, speculation, leverage, diversification and income generation.

There are also some additional benefits you can attain from trading or investing in index options.

Exposure to a broader market

An index represents a large parcel of stocks. Therefore, the index is often representative of the market as a whole, or of a significant segment of the market. Investing in index options allows you to effectively invest in an option that tracks a particular index. This will approximate an investment in that particular parcel of stocks, giving you exposure to a broader market. In this instance, you have the benefit of diversification as your investment does not carry risk attached to specific companies. If one company in the index does not perform well, this may be offset by the general market movement of all the other companies in the index.

You have the benefit of being exposed to the broad market represented by the index, without having to invest in each of the individual stocks that make up that particular index.

Protection for your portfolio

Investors who hold a portfolio of shares may wish to counteract the effect of a market downturn without having to actually sell their shares. Taxation on realisation of the investment gain, plus transaction costs, are two reasons why an investor might consider using options, and in particular index options, to protect their share portfolio.

Buying index put options can provide the investor with some compensation if the market does fall and their portfolio value declines as a result. The increase in the value of their put options will offset the fall in value of their portfolio.

Example 3.1 illustrates how you might use index options to offset a potential fall in the market.

Example 3.1

You own a portfolio of shares that includes some of the larger companies on the stock exchange. Your total portfolio is valued at $50 000. You have experienced some gains on your portfolio recently and expect that the market will have a short correction. You wish to protect the value of your portfolio from this expected price fall.

The value of the market index today is 5000 points, so you decide to purchase a three-month 5000 put option for 50 points.

The index multiplier is $10.

Over the next three months the market falls as you expected and the value of your portfolio is now $45 000. On expiry date, the index is calculated to be 4500 points.

Index value on expiry date	4500 points
Index strike value	5000 points

Index multiplier	$10 per point
Cash value on expiry date	
((5000 points – 4500 points) × $10)	$5 000
Less premium paid (300 points × $10)	$500
Net profit on option	$4 500

This net profit will offset the fall in value of your share portfolio of $5 000.

Chapter summary

⇨ Options can be either call options or put options.

⇨ A call option is the right to buy 100 shares of the underlying stock at the strike price, on or before the expiry date.

⇨ A put option is the right to sell 100 shares of the underlying stock at the strike price, on or before the expiry date.

⇨ Option buyers are speculating that the price of the underlying stock will move sufficiently before the expiry date, in order to generate a profit on the option.

⇨ Option buyers have limited risk. Their total loss on an option contract is limited to the option premium they paid to buy the option.

⇨ Option buyers have the right, but not the obligation, to exercise their option.

⇨ Option sellers charge a premium for granting the right to buy or sell the underlying security.

⇨ Option sellers are generally speculating that the price of the underlying security will move in a way that causes the option to expire worthless or decrease in value.

⇨ A writer of uncovered call options is exposed to unlimited risk as they are exposed to any increase in the market value of the underlying stock.

⇨ A writer of put options is exposed to the value of the underlying stock at the strike price.

⇨ Buyers of call options will generate a profit on their options only if:

  ⌱ the market value of the underlying stock is greater than the strike price

  ⌱ the market value of the underlying stock has risen enough to cover the premium paid and any fall in time value of the option.

⇨ Time is a key factor in determining if an option buyer generates a profit on their trade.

⇨ Buyers of put options will generate a profit on their options only if:

  ⌱ the market value of the underlying stock is less than the strike price

  ⌱ the market value of the underlying stock has fallen enough so that the option price rises enough to cover the premium paid and any fall in time value.

⇨ Company issued options are issued directly by the company and will have specific terms and conditions.

⇨ Index options are options over a stock market index, and can provide a trader or investor with exposure to a broader market.

⇨ Index options are European style options and cash settled on expiry date.

⇨ Index options can be used to gain exposure to a broader market or to protect your stock portfolio against an adverse market movement.

chapter 4

Option pricing

The market forces affecting the value of stocks will in turn affect the market value of the options attached to those stocks. The option itself has no underlying value — its value is derived from the value of the stock and your ability to buy or sell that stock.

In this chapter we will explore the two components of an option price. These components are intrinsic value and time value. We will also look at the factors that affect the price of an option and how these factors vary from the factors that affect the price of a stock.

Stock pricing versus option pricing

Stocks issued by a company are limited in number and as a result their price is influenced by the forces of demand and supply. Like any limited commodity, if more people want to buy a stock than people want to sell, the price will naturally increase. Similarly, if more people wish to sell their stocks and there are few buyers, the stock price will fall. The most extreme example of this is during a stock market crash, or correction, where sellers are flooding the market and, in the absence of any significant buyers, the price falls dramatically.

The reasons why there are more buyers than sellers, or more sellers than buyers, are numerous and varied, and not within the scope of this book. Broadly, the stock price will be influenced by the performance (both actual and expected) of the company and all the economic and industrial factors that affect that actual and expected performance.

With exchange traded options, the exchange will allow investors to buy and sell any number of options. They are not constrained by the number of shares issued of the underlying stock. Therefore, the price of options is affected only indirectly by the forces of supply and demand as they are not a limited commodity.

The option value is primarily affected by the movement in price of the underlying stock and by the passage of time. These factors are referred to as intrinsic value and time value. To add further complexity, different factors will affect the intrinsic value and the time value of any option price.

Tip
Option premium = intrinsic value + time value

Intrinsic value

Intrinsic value is the difference between the market value of the underlying stock and the strike value of the option. This is the most easily understood component of an option price as it represents a defined benefit that can be readily measured.

Tip
Intrinsic value represents the ability to sell an underlying share above the market price (put option), or to buy the underlying share below the current market price (call option).

In-the-money options

Options that have intrinsic value in their pricing are referred to as being 'in-the-money'. For call options, this means that the strike price of the option is below the current market value of the underlying share and so there is value in exercising the option. The intrinsic value is present as the option holder can exercise their option and buy the underlying shares for a price lower than they could on the market. This is illustrated in example 4.1.

Example 4.1

Consider a WBC $20.00 call option that is trading at $1.50. The current market value of WBC is $21.00.

The intrinsic value of this option is $1.00, being the difference between the strike price of the option ($20.00) and the current market price of WBC ($21.00).

The buyer of this option would be able to buy WBC shares at $1.00 below the current market price. These are in-the-money options.

The additional $0.50 in the option price is the time value of the option.

The calculation of intrinsic value in put options is the same as for call options, except that intrinsic value in put option prices is present when the strike price of the option is above the current market value of the underlying stock. The intrinsic value arises as the option holder can exercise their option and sell the underlying shares for a higher price than on the market. This is outlined in example 4.2.

Example 4.2

Consider a WES $35.00 put option that is trading at $2.40. The current market value of WES is $33.40.

Example 4.2 *(cont'd)*

The intrinsic value of this option is the strike price of the option ($35.00) less the current market value of WES ($33.40). This means that this option has an intrinsic value of $1.60 and is in-the-money.

The intrinsic value arises as the option holder is able to sell their shares at a price higher than the current market value.

The remaining $0.80 of value in the option price is time value.

Out-of-the-money options

Options that have no intrinsic value in their pricing are referred to as being 'out-of-the-money'. For call options, this means that the strike price is above the current market value and so there is no value in exercising the option. There is no advantage to buying shares at a price higher than you could pay on the open market. This is explained in example 4.3.

Tip
Call options provide the buyer with the right but not the obligation to buy the underlying shares. If your options are out-of-the-money and you wish to purchase the underlying shares, it is better to buy the shares on the sharemarket directly.

Example 4.3

You have bought a $20.00 call option and the underlying shares are currently trading at $19.50. You option is currently worth $0.20.

Your option has no intrinsic value and the option price represents time value only.

If you wanted to buy the underlying shares, you would purchase them on the sharemarket at $19.50 rather than exercise your option and buy the underlying shares at $20.00.

Tip

Put options provide the buyer with the right but not the obligation to sell the underlying shares. If your options are out-of-the-money and you wish to sell your shares, it is better to sell them on the sharemarket directly.

At-the-money options

As the name suggests, an at-the-money option is an option whereby the strike price of the option is equal to the current market value of the underlying shares. Let's consider this in example 4.4.

Example 4.4

You are considering buying a $35.50 CSL call option as you believe the market price of CSL will rise significantly in the next two months. The current market price of CSL is also $35.50.

These options are at-the-money. The option premium consists of time value only. There is no intrinsic value in at-the-money options.

Time value

Time value is a little more difficult to comprehend than intrinsic value. Time value is the amount you are prepared to pay for the possibility that the market will move in your favour during the life of an option so that you will profit on your purchase.

Time value in options will vary with in-the-money, out-of-the-money and at-the-money options. This is because each of these scenarios presents different opportunities and possibilities of an increase in intrinsic value of an option. Generally, time value is greatest on at-the-money options, as this presents an opportunity for building intrinsic value into the option if the market moves in the right direction.

Tip

The further the strike price is from the market value of the underlying stock, the less time value the option will have.

Time value is influenced by the following factors:

⇨ time to expiry

⇨ volatility

⇨ interest rates

⇨ dividend payments

⇨ market expectations.

Time to expiry

The most obvious factor affecting the time value of an option is time itself. As time value represents the possibility of a market movement in your favour, it follows that the more time you have in which to achieve this market movement, the greater the chance is of it happening. Thus, the longer the time period left on an option contract, the greater the time value will be.

As the time draws closer to the expiry date on your option, the opportunity for your option to increase in value reduces, and hence the time value of your option reduces. This reduction in time value over the life of an option is called time decay.

Time decay is not a linear variable. That is, the time value contained within an option price does not reduce at a constant rate. Time value actually reduces at a faster rate as you get closer to the expiry date.

Figure 4.1 illustrates the time value held in a typical option over the life of the option.

Figure 4.1: time value

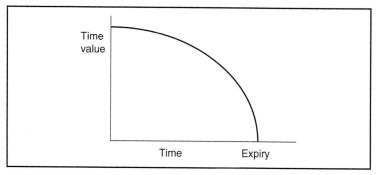

Tip

When choosing the expiry month of your option, you need to weigh up the cost of the option (which will be greater with more time to expiry) with the time needed for your strategy to work in your favour.

Volatility

Volatility is the range and speed in which a price moves. When a price moves by a large amount within a short space of time, it is said to have high volatility.

An option buyer is looking for the price of the underlying share to move by a sufficient amount in order to make a profit on the option. Therefore, it follows that the volatility, or the range and speed in which the underlying stock moves, will affect the price of the option.

The greater the volatility of the underlying share, the greater the time value of the option. Consider an option that is currently out-of-the-money. If the underlying share price normally moves in a large range within a short space of time, it is more likely that the option will move into the money and create value for the buyer. As time value represents the possibility of the market moving in your direction, it follows that options over shares with higher volatility will contain a higher time value.

Interest rates

When you buy a call option, you have the advantage of leverage as you only need to pay a fraction of the cost of the underlying stock to be exposed to movements in the price of that stock. Compared with buying the underlying stock, you will have additional funds that you are able to invest elsewhere. When interest rates rise, this benefit increases as you would earn a higher rate on these funds. For this reason, when interest rates rise, call option premiums will also increase in value.

When you buy a put option, you are effectively delaying the sale of your underlying stock until you exercise the option. Put another way, you are deferring the time at which you receive payment for the sale of your stock until you exercise your option. If you sold your stock immediately, you would have those funds to invest elsewhere. Therefore, when interest rates rise, put option premiums fall as this delay in receiving funds now carries a higher opportunity cost.

Tip

A rise in interest rates will cause the premium of call options to rise and cause the premium on put options to fall.

Dividend payments

When a company declares a dividend payable to shareholders, it announces both an ex-dividend date and the dividend payment date. When trading options, it is the ex-dividend date that is important. The ex-dividend date is the day on which all shareholders who own the appropriate class of shares at the end of trade on that day will be entitled to the dividend payment. The next day, the share price usually falls by an amount similar to the dividend amount, as anyone who buys shares on that day will not be entitled to the dividend. The dividend will be payable to the owner of the shares on the ex-dividend date, regardless of whether they still own the shares on the payment date.

Tip

Most major companies announce and pay dividends at a similar time each year and often at similar amounts. They will also provide earnings updates and other information to allow investors to estimate the timing and amount of potential dividends.

Options do not grant you any rights to dividends in the underlying shares. It is therefore important to consider any upcoming dividend announcements or ex-dividend dates when selecting and pricing options. If the underlying share has an ex-dividend date during the life of an option, this will affect the intrinsic value of the option, without the option holder having any rights to any dividends. For this reason, any expected dividend announcements will be built into the option premium.

Market expectations

Ultimately, it is the expectations of buyers and sellers that determine the market value of options. If the buyers and sellers have an expectation of a certain movement in the market price of the underlying shares, this will be built into the price of any option premiums.

Pricing models

As we have already outlined in this chapter, there are many factors that will influence the premium price of an option. You need to consider the strike price, the price and volatility of the underlying stock, the time left to expiry, expected dividends and interest rates in calculating the fair value of an option. An option pricing model is a formula that combines all of these factors to calculate a fair value for you.

Option pricing models are used by traders and investors to assist them to determine if options are priced at a fair value in the market. It is important to note that the 'fair value' calculated by a pricing model may not be the current market price or the price quoted on the market by market makers. You still need to match a willing buyer and a willing seller to buy and sell an option.

Tip

You do not need to be an expert on option pricing models to use one. An understanding of how they work is enough to be able to use an option pricing model to estimate fair value of an option.

The ASX provides a theoretical option price calculator on its website that you can use to calculate a fair value for an option. The calculator will also provide you with estimates for all of the variables, including dividend and volatility, which you can adjust.

Some of the factors that influence an option price are known, including the strike price, market price of the underlying stock and the time to expiry. However, other factors, such as expected dividends, interest rate changes and in particular the volatility of the underlying stock, also need to be estimated to calculate a fair value. Therefore, two investors using the same pricing model may still calculate a different fair value for the same option if their assumptions about volatility and dividends are different.

Estimating volatility

In estimating the volatility of the underlying stock, you need to consider both the historical volatility and the implied volatility.

Historical volatility uses the price range of the underlying stock over a recent period and measures the actual volatility over this period. If you are using historical volatility, you are assuming that the underlying stock will continue to behave in a similar fashion over the life of the option.

The current market price of an option will have been based on the market view of the expected volatility of the underlying stock over the life of the option. Although this will most likely be based on historical volatility, other expectations will be built into this estimation. The value inherent in the current market price of the option is called implied volatility.

Fair value versus market value

Based on your estimates of dividends, forecast interest rates and volatility, you are able to use an option pricing calculator to determine what you feel is the fair value for an option. You then need to decide if you wish to enter into an option transaction at the current market price. If you feel that an option is mispriced in the market, you can implement a trading strategy to profit from this opportunity.

In general terms, if you assess that an option is overvalued (usually as the implied volatility is too high), then strategies involving writing options may suit as you have assessed that the option premiums are currently too high. Alternatively, if you assess that an option is undervalued (the implied volatility is too low), then strategies involving buying options will allow you to buy options you consider are priced below their fair value.

Delta

Delta is a value that measures how an option moves in response to a movement in the price of the underlying stock. If the underlying stock moves by $1, will the option premium move by exactly $1, or less than $1?

Tip

Delta is shown as a number between zero and one, or shown as a percentage.

You use the following formula to determine the change in price of an option in reaction to a change in value of the underlying stock:

Delta × change in price of the underlying stock
= change in the price of the option

We use this formula in example 4.5.

Example 4.5

Assume your option has a delta of 0.8 (or 80 per cent) and the underlying stock moves in price by $1.

You would expect that your option will move in price by $0.80 (0.8 × $1).

The distance of the strike price of the option to the current market price of the underlying stock will affect the delta of an option. The following guidelines are an indication of the delta you will usually find attached to options with different strike prices:

⇨ An at-the-money option, where the market value of the underlying stock is equal to the strike price, will have a delta of approximately 0.5.

⇨ The further an option is out-of-the-money, the closer the delta of the option will be to zero.

⇨ An option that is deep in-the-money (e.g. a call option where the market value of the underlying stock is well above the strike price) will have a delta closer to one.

Tip

Options over the same underlying stock but with different strike prices will have different deltas.

Pay-off diagrams

Regardless of the strategy you decide to use when trading options, you should always be aware of the key price levels at which you will break even, make a profit or make a loss. You should also be aware of the risks involved in the strategy you use and the potential losses to which you may be exposed.

Pay-off diagrams can be used to illustrate these levels so that you can readily refer to them. A pay-off diagram will show you the intrinsic value of your option based on the price of the underlying security. It shows you the potential profit or loss you will make on your option position, excluding transaction costs, in relation to the market value of the underlying stock at expiry. It will also show you the break-even point, before transaction costs, for your option trade.

A pay-off diagram, also called a break-even diagram, can be drawn for any option or even a combination of options within the same class. The break-even point is the price of the underlying stock at which you will make neither a profit nor a loss on your option position at expiry (excluding transaction costs).

Tip

Pay-off (break-even) diagrams do not take into account your transaction costs. You need to account for these costs to determine your true profit or loss on your option trade.

For the remaining discussion on pay-off diagrams, we will ignore transaction costs to simplify the examples. To include these costs in your diagrams, simply add your expected transaction costs to your option premium (if an option buyer) or deduct them from your option premium (if an option seller).

Call option buyer

For a buyer of call options, you will break even on your option position at expiry when the intrinsic value of your option is equal to the premium you paid. Therefore, the break-even point will always be the strike price plus the option premium you paid.

Referring to figure 4.2, assume you have bought a $34 CSL call option for $2. The break-even point for your option at expiry will be $36. At $36 your option will have an intrinsic value of $2 that will offset the $2 option premium you paid. When the market value is above $36, you will make a profit. When the market value is between $34 (strike price) and $36, you will make a loss. If the market value of CSL is $34 or below, your loss will be equal to the $2 premium you paid.

Figure 4.2 shows that when CSL is at or below the strike price of $34, the option buyer makes a loss of $2, being the option premium paid. As the price of CSL rises above $34, the loss is reduced up to the break-even point at $36. Above $36, the option has enough intrinsic value to cover the premium paid and the option holder will make a profit. This does not take into account any transaction costs.

Figure 4.2: pay-off diagram — buyer of CSL call options

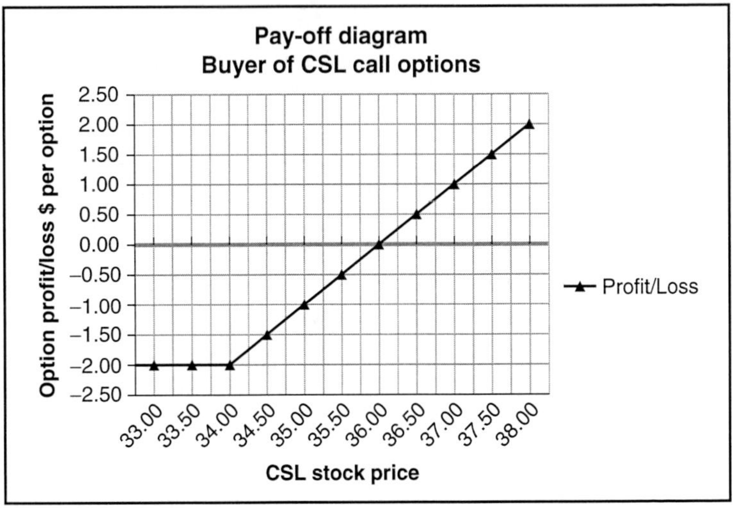

Call option writer

For a writer of call options, you will break even on your option position at expiry when the intrinsic value of the option you sold is equal to the premium you received. Therefore, the break-even point will always be the strike price plus the option premium you received.

> *Tip*
> *The break-even point for a call option buyer will be the strike price of the option plus the option premium. This is the same break-even point for a call option writer.*

Referring to figure 4.3 (overleaf), assume you have sold a $34 CSL call option for $2. The break-even point for your option at expiry will be $36. At $36 your option will have an intrinsic value of $2 that will offset your option premium of $2, leaving you with a net zero position. When the market value is above $36, you will make a loss on selling your option. Your loss will be equal to the difference between the market value of CSL and the strike price of $34, less the $2 premium received. Potentially, this loss has no limit as it will increase as long as the market price of the underlying stock increases. When the market value of CSL is at or below the strike price of $34 you will make a profit of $2, being the premium you received on selling the option. When the market value is between $34 (strike price) and $36, your profit will gradually reduce to zero.

Figure 4.3 shows that the option writer retains their option premium of $2 as profit if the market value of CSL is at or below $34. This profit is eroded to zero as the market price of CSL moves from $34 to $36. When the market price of CSL is above $36, the option writer will make a loss.

Figure 4.3: pay-off diagram — writer of CSL call options

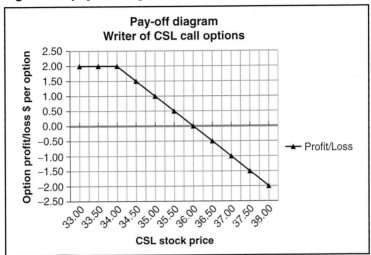

Pay-off diagrams represent the profit and loss based on the intrinsic value of the option only. They only apply to the market price at expiry when there is no time value left in the option price.

Tip

If you want to include your transaction costs in your pay-off diagram, simply add your transaction costs to your option premium and then calculate your break-even point.

Put option buyer

Pay-off diagrams can be drawn in the same way as for call options. A key difference is that the break-even point on a put option position at expiry will be equal to the strike price *less* the option premium.

We will use figure 4.4 to illustrate. Assume you have bought a $41 WPL put option for $2. You are expecting the market value of WPL to fall and wish to benefit from this movement.

Figure 4.4: pay-off diagram — buyer of WPL put options

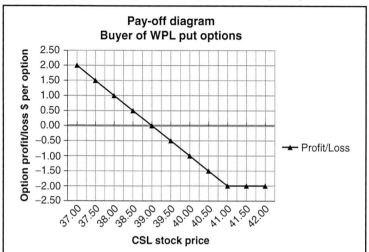

In figure 4.4 you can see that the break-even point for your put option at expiry will be $39. At $39 your option will have an intrinsic value of $2 that will offset the $2 option premium you paid. When the market value is below $39, you will make a profit. When the market value is between $41 (strike price) and $39, you will make a loss. If the market value of WPL is $41 or above, your loss will be equal to the $2 premium you paid.

Put option writer

For a writer of put options, as with a seller of put options, the break-even point will always be the strike price less the option premium. In figure 4.5 (overleaf) we will use the example of a $41 WPL put option that you have sold for $2.

Figure 4.5: pay-off diagram — writer of WPL put options

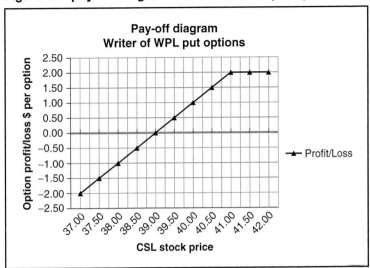

In figure 4.5 you can see that the break-even point for your put option at expiry will be $39. At $39 your option will have an intrinsic value of $2 that will offset the $2 option premium you received. When the market value is below $39, you will make a loss. When the market value is between $41 (strike price) and $39, you will make a profit. If the market value of WPL is $41 or above, your profit will be equal to the $2 premium you received.

Tip

The break-even point for the put option buyer will be the strike price of the option less the option premium. This is the same break-even point for a put option writer.

Chapter summary

⇨ As options are not a limited commodity, they are less influenced by the forces of supply and demand that determine market prices for shares.

⇨ The number of options bought and sold is not limited by the exchange.

⇨ Intrinsic value is the difference between the market value of the underlying stock and the strike price of the option.

⇨ Intrinsic value represents the ability to sell an underlying share above the market price, or to buy the underlying share below the current market price.

⇨ Call options have intrinsic value if the market value of the underlying shares is higher than the strike price of the option.

⇨ Put options have intrinsic value when the market value of the underlying shares is lower than the strike price of the option.

⇨ In-the-money options are options that have intrinsic value in the option premium.

⇨ Out-of-the-money options do not have any intrinsic value in the option premium.

⇨ At-the-money options are options where the market value of the underlying share is equal to the strike price.

⇨ You would be unlikely to exercise an out-of-the-money option as this would result in selling the underlying shares below the current market price (put options) or buying the underlying shares above the current market price (call options).

⇨ Time value is the amount you are prepared to pay for the possibility that the market will move in your favour during the life of the option.

⇨ Time value in options is influenced by:

ф time to expiry

ф volatility

ф interest rates

ф dividend payments

ф market expectations.

⇨ The longer the time period remaining on an option, the greater the possibility of the option creating a profit for the buyer and the greater the time value in the option premium.

⇨ The greater the volatility of the underlying share price, the greater the time value of any options over those shares.

⇨ Any expected change in interest rates during the life of the option should be factored into the premium price.

⇨ It is important to consider any expected ex-dividend date that may fall during the life of an option as this needs to be factored into the premium price.

⇨ Option pricing models are formulas that take into account all the factors affecting an option premium to calculate a fair value of the option.

⇨ The fair value calculated is dependent on the assumptions used in the option pricing model, including estimated volatility, dividends and interest rates. Two different investors may calculate a different fair value for the same option if they use different assumptions.

⇨ Estimating volatility of the underlying stock price is a key variable in using option pricing models to calculate fair value.

⇨ Delta is a value that measures how the price of an option moves in relation to movement in the underlying stock.

⇨ Delta is a number between 0 and 1.

⇨ Pay-off diagrams represent your profit or loss on your option trade based on the intrinsic value of the option only. They show the profit or loss at expiry.

⇨ Pay-off diagrams can be constructed for any option position.

⇨ The break-even point at expiry for a call option is the strike price of the underlying stock plus the option premium paid or received.

⇨ The break-even point at expiry for a put option is the strike price of the underlying stock less the option premium paid or received.

chapter 5

The mechanics: how to buy, sell and exercise options

In this chapter we will look at the mechanics of trading options, how to open a position and how you can then close your open position if you wish to. We will also look at how you sell options and the margin requirements that are attached to selling options.

Towards the end of this chapter we discuss the additional documentation requirements you need to complete to trade options with your broker and how this may affect the option strategies your broker will allow you to undertake with them. Our last topic is market makers. We discuss who they are and what they do.

Opening a position

As we outlined in chapter 1, you must specify or select the four standard terms of your option before you can buy or sell an option. The four standard terms (strike price, the expiry date, the underlying stock and if you are trading a put option or a call option) are set by the exchange. For each underlying stock, there will be a range or series of put and call options available that have various strike prices and expiry dates. A complete list of all the options is available from the exchange and also from most brokers.

Whenever you enter an option trade by either buying or selling an option, it is referred to as opening a trade. If you sold an option, it is an opening sale, and if you bought an option, it is an opening purchase. Your option position, either as a purchaser or a seller, is referred to as an open position.

Tip

The total number of open contracts in a particular type of option is referred to as the open interest.

Options are listed on the exchange the same way in which shares are listed. The options are listed by their code, with a bid price and an ask price. The bid price is the price at which someone is willing to buy this particular option, and the ask price is the price at which someone is willing to sell the option.

If you wish to buy an option, you would place your order through your broker, just as you would to buy a share. If you wish to sell an option, you would also place your sale order through your broker. All options trades are executed on the market in priority of price and time. The best priced order will be executed first and if there is more than one order entered at the same price, the order placed on the market first will take priority.

You are able to place both market and limit orders for options. A market order is an order to buy or sell at the best price currently available on the market. A limit order is an order to buy or sell at a specific price only.

If you currently have an open position that is nearing its expiry date, you may wish to continue to hold that position by closing your current position and opening a new option position on a similar option with a later expiry date. This is referred to as rolling over your position. It is possible to use a combination order to execute both of these trades in a single order. You can specify the net price at which you wish to roll over your position but you do not need to specify a price for each leg of the trade. If the order goes through, both the close of your initial position and the opening of a new position will be executed at the same time. This avoids the risk of a market move against you in the time it might take to execute both positions individually.

Tip

It is important to note that all option orders on the ASX are good for day orders. This means that any orders that have not been filled at the end of the trading day will be deleted. If you still wish to place your order the next day, you will need to place a new order in the morning.

Closing a position

To close your option position, you simply place an order to cancel out your open position. If you had purchased an option, to close your option position you would place an order to sell the same type and amount of the option contract.

Options clearing

The settlement and clearing functions for the options market are quite different from the sharemarket. On the sharemarket, all the trades are executed between a specific buyer and seller and settlement of the trade occurs three trading days later. In Australia, the ASX performs the functions of both trades and settlement.

Options are traded on the ASX; however, a separate organisation, ASX Clear, is responsible for the settlement function. This requires ASX Clear to both clear all options that are traded on the ASX and ensure that all contractual obligations relating to options are met. For instance, if an option holder wishes to exercise their option, ASX Clear is responsible for ensuring that they assign this to an option seller and that the seller meets this obligation.

When you place an option order through your broker, your broker becomes your trading participant and is responsible for registering your trade with the ASX. When the trade is executed, a contract is created between your broker and the other party's broker. This contract is called the market contract. At this point, a process of novation occurs in which the market contract is replaced by two separate contracts as follows:

⇨ a contract between your broker and ASX Clear

⇨ a contract between the other party's broker and ASX Clear.

Under this process of novation, ASX Clear becomes the counterparty to all open option positions. This means that you no longer have any relationship with the original counterparty to your option contract. As an option buyer, you do not need to assess the credit risk of the seller and their ability to meet their obligations if you decide to exercise or sell your option. Let's have a look at this process in figure 5.1.

Tip

Buying or selling an option creates a contract between parties. Unlike when you buy or sell shares, there is no transfer of ownership or title to the underlying shares.

Figure 5.1: buying and selling options

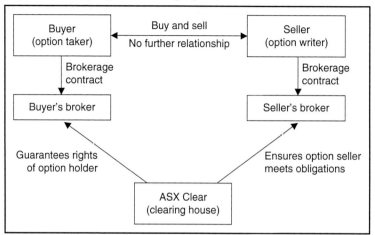

Option settlement

As we have just outlined, ASX Clear is responsible for the settlement of all option contracts. Settlement for options contracts occurs one business day after the trade date. This is often referred to as T+1 (where T stands for transaction day). This is different from share transactions, which settle on the third business day after the transaction and are referred to as T+3.

Tip

If you buy an option contract, you must pay your premium one business day after you buy it. If you sell an option, you will receive your premium one business day after you have sold it.

Exercising an option

If you wish to exercise your option, you need to notify your broker who is required to submit an exercise notice to ASX Clear. When ASX Clear receives an exercise notice, it will randomly select a writer who has sold the same type of option and will assign the exercise to the writer.

Tip

It is too late to close out your position once ASX Clear has assigned an exercise notice to an option you have sold.

When an option is exercised, the transaction is settled three business days after the option is exercised; that is, T+3. This is in line with settlement for stocks. The reason for this is so that the option writer is able to buy the underlying stock from the market (which settles T+3) if they need to in order to comply with the exercise of a call option and they do not currently hold that stock.

If you exercise your call option, you will pay for and receive the underlying shares three business days after exercise. If you have sold a call option that is exercised, you will receive payment for the shares at the strike price and must deliver the shares three business days after the exercise.

Tip

Option contracts are settled T+1.
Exercise of options are settled T+3.

If you do not exercise an in-the-money option before the expiry date, it will expire worthless, regardless of how much intrinsic value might be attached to that option. To avoid this, you need to ensure that you monitor your option positions and either sell or exercise your options before the expiry date.

It is possible to set your trading account to auto-exercise, so that your options will automatically be exercised if they are in-the-money at expiry. This is particularly useful for cash settled index options, as exercise of the option always results in a cash payment rather than delivery of an underlying share.

Trading costs

Brokerage will be payable on any option orders that are executed. Brokerage rates will vary between brokers and may be payable at a flat rate or as a percentage based on the option premium, or a combination of both a flat rate and a percentage. You will need to check with individual brokers to determine the brokerage rates and structure that will best suit you. ASX Clear also charges a fee per contract, which may be included in your brokerage or may be charged to you separately by your broker.

Tip

You will also pay an exercise fee if you wish to exercise your option. For costs, check with your broker.

Margins

When you write an option contract, you have a potential obligation to deliver the underlying shares if that option is exercised. As an option writer you may also have potentially unlimited risk if the market moves against your position. In order to ensure you can meet this obligation, ASX Clear requires all option writers to provide a margin.

Tip

You only need to provide a margin if you sell an option contract. Option buyers do not need to provide any margin for their open positions.

ASX Clear calculates the amount of security that it deems necessary to ensure that the option writer can meet their obligations under the option contract. As the option contract value is affected by the market price of the underlying stock, the value of any margin requirement will also change as the market price of the underlying stock changes.

ASX Clear calculates the margin requirements using a system known as the ASX Derivatives Margining System (ADMS). This calculates the margin requirement using a set formula that takes into account the current option premium and the volatility of the underlying security.

The margin required for options consists of two components:

⇨ a premium margin

⇨ a risk margin.

The premium margin is the value of the premium attached to your option at the close of each day. This is basically the amount you would need to close out your option position by buying the same type of option.

The risk margin is designed to cover the potential movement in the premium margin in any given day. This is calculated by reference to the usual intraday movement in price of the underlying share. This movement is referred to as the daily volatility. The daily volatility is expressed as a percentage and known as the margin interval. The ASX publishes and updates the margin interval for all option classes each week.

Tip

Your margin requirement will be calculated on your entire portfolio of open option contracts, so that some positions may offset the margin requirements of other positions on a daily basis.

As you know, due to the process of novation, ASX Clear has a contract with your broker in relation to your option contract, rather than with you directly. ASX Clear will impose the margin on your broker, who will in turn require you to provide them with a margin for your option contract. You should be aware that your broker may assess your margin risk differently to ASX Clear and require a larger margin than that calculated under ADMS.

How to pay your margin

If you sell an option, you will need to provide either cash or other collateral to cover your margin. The other collateral usually includes shares you own or bank guarantees. If you are providing shares as collateral, your broker may require more than your margin to insure against any adverse falls in those share values.

Generally, your broker will set up a separate options account where they will hold your margin, including the premium you received on selling the option contract. They will then transfer shares or cash between your trading account and your options account as required in order to cover your margin. When you close your option contract and it has been settled, they will transfer the value of your options account back to your trading account.

When your margin increases and you do not have the available funds in your trading account, you will receive a margin call from your broker. This will require you to deposit additional funds or security to cover the margin within a set time frame, usually 24 hours. If you are unable to or fail to meet a margin call, your broker may close out your option positions without further reference to you.

Opening an options account

In order to buy or write options, you will need to open an options account with your broker. You will need to sign an Options Client Agreement, which is in addition to the brokerage agreement you need for a share trading account with your broker.

As part of the process of setting up to trade options, your broker is required to determine your suitability for this type of trading strategy. It is likely they will ask you to complete a questionnaire to assess whether options are an appropriate investment for you. You may be asked for details about your investment experience, financial position, risk tolerance, knowledge of options and your financial objectives in trading options. Your broker may restrict the strategies you are able to trade through them based on your answers to those questions.

Market makers

The ASX will set up many individual series of options that are available for investors and traders to buy and sell. However, there may not always be retail traders providing a bid and ask price for every individual option. Market makers are the financial institutions who can provide bids and offers on the market so that investors and traders can buy and sell options for which there is not a retail counterparty. Having market makers provide these bids and asks also assists with valuing an option position.

There is no difference for you if you buy from or sell to a market maker than if you buy from or sell to a retail investor. In fact, you will not know if your option trade is with a market maker or a retail investor.

Market makers are financial institutions that operate as professional traders and usually trade a wide range of financial instruments. They receive a fee from the ASX to provide the bid and ask prices for options. They are required to meet requirements on the number of contracts offered, the spread between the bid and ask price, and the period over which they offer these contracts.

The spread is the difference between the bid price (price at which the market maker is willing to buy an option) and the ask price (price at which the market maker is willing to sell an option).

It is important for you to consider the spread as a cost of your option strategy. Throughout this book we refer to option examples with the market value of the option being a specific price. In reality, there will be a price to buy the option and a price to sell the option. The distance between these prices will add to the cost of any option strategy.

Tip

The tighter the spread (less difference between the ask and bid prices), the better for you as an investor. A large spread means that it will cost you more to exit your position.

Market makers are not required to provide a market all day every day. There is no guarantee that the option you wish to trade will have a price and quantity available to trade. Certain events, such as company announcements, high volatility in the underlying stock or low liquidity in the underlying stock, will affect when market makers provide their bid and ask quotes. However, if a quote is not available for the option you wish to trade, you are able to request a quote from the market maker through your broker. Even still, it is prudent to have a plan if the market maker does not provide a quote for your option, particularly if you need to close an open option position.

Chapter summary

⇨ To open an option position, you simply place your order with your broker as you would for a share transaction.

⇨ Entering an option trade as either a buyer or a seller is referred to as opening an option position.

⇨ You can place both market and limit orders for options.

⇨ You can place a combination order to effect a sale and purchase simultaneously if you wish to roll over your option position past the current expiry date.

⇨ To close your option position you place an order that cancels out your opening option transaction.

⇨ Options are traded on the ASX with a settlement time frame of T+1.

⇨ ASX Clear is responsible for settlement of all option contracts and ensuring that option writers fulfil the obligations under their option contracts.

⇨ ASX Clear has a contract with your broker, not you, through a process of novation whenever you open an option position.

⇨ To exercise your option, you need to notify your broker who will then lodge an exercise notice with ASX Clear.

⇨ ASX Clear randomly assigns the exercise to an option writer. You cannot close your option position after assignment.

⇨ Exercise of option contracts occurs three business days after the exercise date (T+3).

⇨ If you do not close out or exercise your option, it will expire worthless, regardless of any intrinsic value it might have.

⇨ Writers of options are required to provide a margin to ensure they are able to meet their option obligations.

⇨ Margins are calculated using the premium value and the daily volatility of the underlying shares.

⇨ Margins include a premium margin and a risk margin.

⇨ You can meet your margin by providing cash, shares or bank guarantees.

⇨ You will need to sign an options client agreement with your broker in order to buy or write options.

⇨ Market makers are financial institutions that provide bid and ask prices for individual series of options.

chapter 6

Buying options: the scenarios

In this chapter we will look at the different scenarios that are possible when buying either a put option or a call option.

At the end of this chapter you should have a good understanding of how changes in price of the underlying stock will affect the value of your option and what alternative courses of action you can take based on this price movement.

Buying options

When buying options you are speculating that the market price of the underlying stock will move in your direction by a large enough amount to generate a profit on your option. If you are right, your percentage returns are significant. However, if you are wrong, you can potentially lose the entire premium you paid for the option.

The actions to take after purchasing your option will be determined by three factors:

⇨ *The price movement of the underlying stock and the effect this has on the value of your option.* It is of particular significance if this price movement results in your option being in-the-money and holding some intrinsic value.

⇨ *Your reasons for buying the option and the outcomes you were trying to achieve or protect against.* We explore specific option strategies in the later chapters of this book.

⇨ *Your risk tolerance.* This is your ability to hold an option as it approaches the expiry date with the expectation of a price movement within a short period of time and an increasing rate of time decay.

We will now take you through the scenarios that you potentially face as a buyer of a call option and a buyer of a put option.

Buying a call option

Remember that when buying a call option, you are buying the *right* to buy the underlying stock. You are not obligated to exercise your call option and actually buy the stock. However, if you do wish to exercise your option and acquire the underlying stock at the exercise price, you must do this before the option expires. If you do not wish to buy the underlying stock but still wish to generate a profit from your option, you can also sell your option before the expiry date.

Let's now examine the various scenarios that can arise when you purchase a call option and the courses of action that are available to you under each scenario. Let's begin with example 6.1.

Example 6.1

Assume you believe the market price of XYZ stock will rise by $1.00 in the next month and you want to profit from this increase.

Current market value of XYZ	$25.00
Date today	1 April
Call option price	$1.50
Exercise price	$24.00
Expiry month*	May

You decide to buy three XYZ call options at $1.50 each.

* Remember the expiry date is the Thursday before the last Friday in the month.

In example 6.1, your three XYZ call options will cost you $450.00 (three contracts at $1.50 per share multiplied by 100 shares per contract). By purchasing these options, you now have the right to purchase 300 shares in XYZ for the exercise price of $24.00. You are able to exercise this right at any time between now and the option expiry at the end of May.

There are a number of actions you may take depending on the movement in the market price of XYZ. We will examine each of these based on the following three scenarios:

⇨ The market value of XYZ increases.

⇨ The market value of XYZ does not change.

⇨ The market value of XYZ decreases.

Scenario 1: the market value of XYZ increases

You have purchased in-the-money options. If the market value of the underlying stock, XYZ, increases, the value of your call option will also increase by a similar amount.

Let's say that XYZ has increased in market value by $1.50 to $26.50 in the four weeks since you bought your call option. The market value of your call option is now $2.80. This increase of $1.30 is represented by the $1.50 increase in value of the underlying stock (XYZ), less a decrease in the time value of $0.20. Our scenario can be now summarised in example 6.2.

Example 6.2

The market value of XYZ has increased from $25.00 to $26.50 since you purchased your call options.

Current market value of XYZ	$26.50
Date today	1 May
Expiry month	May
Call option cost	$1.50
Exercise price	$24.00
Call option current value	$2.80

You have three alternative courses of action.

⇨ Exercise your options and buy the shares at the exercise price of $24.00, $2.50 below the current market value.

⇨ Sell your options at a profit.

⇨ Hold your options longer, in the expectation of a further increase in the market price of XYZ and then take the first or second action in this list.

Exercise your options

If you wish to purchase the 300 shares in XYZ, you can exercise your options and pay $24.00 per share. You will be purchasing your shares at $2.50 below the current market value.

Your total profit on this transaction (excluding transaction costs) would be as follows:

Current market value of XYZ ($26.50 × 300 shares)	$7950.00
Cost price of XYZ ($24.00 × 300 shares)	($7200.00)
Premium paid for the option	($450.00)
Net profit*	$300.00

* This ignores your transaction costs, which must be factored in to your analysis.

On your investment of $450.00, you have made a net profit of $300.00. This was achieved based on a 6 per cent rise in the value of the underlying stock. This is an unrealised profit as it is based on the current market price of $26.50, which may change.

Sell your options

Your second course of action is to sell your call options and realise a profit on sale. Your call options are currently worth $2.80. Your total profit on this transaction would be as follows:

Sale price of XYZGA ($2.80 × 3 contracts × 100 shares)	$840.00
Premium paid for the option	($450.00)
Net profit*	$390.00

* This ignores your transaction costs, which must be factored in to your analysis.

You will notice that your profit on sale of the call options is $90.00 higher than if you exercise your options and purchase the actual shares. The difference is due to the time value contained in the option premium. At a price of $2.80, the option has an intrinsic value of $2.50 (due to market value of the underlying shares being $2.50 above the exercise price of $24.00), plus a time value of $0.30 (representing the time value from today until the expiry date). In selling your options, you are also selling this extra $0.30 of time value, as the following formula reveals:

$0.30 × 3 contracts × 100 shares per contract = $90

Hold your options

Your third course of action is to hold your options. You would do this if your expectation was that the price of XYZ will continue to increase, which would result in a higher value of your options. It is important to note that the time value of your options will decrease at a faster rate the closer you get to the expiry date, so your expectation must be that the shares will increase in excess of the time value left in the option premium.

You would still need to take action to either exercise your option or sell your option before the expiry date. If you fail to sell or exercise your options, they will expire worthless, even if they have intrinsic value on expiry.

Scenario 2: the market value of XYZ does not change

If the market value of your underlying stock, XYZ, does not change or only changes by a small amount, the value of your call option will not increase. In fact, the value of your call option will decrease due to the reduction in time value as you near the expiry date. Our scenario can be now summarised in example 6.3.

Example 6.3

The market value of XYZ has not moved from $25.00 since you purchased your call options.

Current market value of XYZ	$25.00
Date today	1 May
Expiry month	May
Call option cost	$1.50
Exercise price	$24.00
Call option current value	$1.30

You have three alternative courses of action.

⇨ Exercise your options and buy the shares at the exercise price of $24.00, $1.50 below the current market value.

⇨ Sell your options.

⇨ Hold your options longer, in the expectation that the market price of XYZ will increase and then take the first or second action in this list.

Exercise your options

If you wish to purchase the 300 shares in XYZ, you can exercise your options and pay $24 per share for a total of $7200 for your 300 shares. You will be purchasing your shares at $1 below the market value.

At the current market value, your total loss on this transaction would be as follows:

Current market value of XYZ ($25 × 300 shares)	$7500
Cost price of XYZ ($24 × 300 shares)	($7200)
Premium paid for the option	($450)
Net loss*	($150)

* This ignores your transaction costs, which must be factored in to your analysis.

You paid $450.00 for the right to purchase 300 XYZ shares at $1.50 below their current market value. Remember that this is a right, not an obligation, and you are not obligated to buy these shares unless you want to by exercising your call option.

Although this transaction appears to have resulted in a loss, in this example it is important to understand your trading strategy in this circumstance. In exercising the option, you have decided to purchase the stock. Given that the price has not increased, you must have another reason for wanting to purchase this stock. Most likely, this reason will be that you are still expecting a rise in the stock price;

however, this rise was not achieved within the time deadline of your call option. Or perhaps you may have been satisfied to pay $150 as the cost of insuring against an expected price increase in this stock to enable you to delay your initial purchase date.

Sell your options

Your second course of action is to sell your call options. Your call options are currently worth $1.30. Your total loss on this transaction would be as follows:

Sale price of XYZ ($1.30 × 3 contracts × 100 shares)	$390.00
Premium paid for the option	($450.00)
Net loss*	($60.00)

* This ignores your transaction costs, which must be factored in to your analysis.

Your decision to sell your options at this point in time is based on your expectation of the movement in price of the underlying stock. If you no longer believe that the underlying stock value will increase, and you do not wish to own the stock, then selling your options would be a reasonable course of action. Holding the options to expiry, in the absence of any increase in the market value of XYZ, would result in a further reduction in the value of your call options.

Hold your options

Your third course of action is to hold your options. You would do this if your expectation was that the price of XYZ will increase by more than $0.30 before expiry, to offset the fall in time value of the options (currently $0.30) and result in a higher value of your options. It is important to note that the time value of your options will decrease at a faster rate the closer you get to the expiry date.

You may also wish to hold your options longer if your reason for purchasing them was to lock in the price of $24 to acquire the underlying XYZ shares at a date closer to the expiry date of the options.

You would still need to take action to either exercise your options or sell your options before the expiry date.

Scenario 3: the market value of XYZ decreases

If the market value of the underlying stock XYZ decreases, the value of your call option will also decrease due to a fall in both intrinsic value and time value. Let's say that XYZ has decreased in market value by $1.50 to $23.50 in the four weeks since you bought your call option. The market value of your call option is now $0.30. As the market value of the underlying stock is below the strike price, the option has no intrinsic value. The $0.30 represents time value, or the possibility that the price of XYZ will rise above the strike price of $24.00 before expiry and your option will increase in value. Our scenario can be now summarised in example 6.4.

Example 6.4

The market value of XYZ has decreased from $25.00 to $23.50 since you purchased your call options.

Current market value of XYZ	$23.50
Date today	1 May
Expiry month	May
Call option cost	$1.50
Exercise price	$24.00
Call option current value	$0.30

You have three alternative courses of action.

⇨ Sell your options at a loss now.

⇨ Hold your options longer, in the expectation that the market price of XYZ will rise more than $0.30 above the strike price before the expiry date.

⇨ Let your options expire worthless.

You would not exercise your options, as this would result in purchasing XYZ at $24.00, $0.50 higher than you could purchase the shares directly.

Sell your options

Your first alternative is to sell your call options at their current price of $0.30. You would do this if you no longer held an expectation that the market value of XYZ was going to rise by more than $0.30 above the strike price (to at least $24.30) before the expiry date.

Hold your options

Your second course of action is to hold your options. You would do this if your expectation was that the price of XYZ will increase by more than $0.80 before the expiry date. You need the market value of the underlying shares to increase in price by enough to offset the remaining time decay and to put your option in-the-money. In this example, this equates to $0.30 time value and $0.50 to bring the option into the money, resulting in a minimum $0.80 move before expiry to make a profit on the option.

If you hold on to the options and the market value of XYZ fails to move above the strike price before expiry date, your options will expire worthless.

Let your options expire worthless

As your options are only worth $0.30, it may cost you more in transaction fees to sell them than to simply let them expire worthless.

Tip

When selling options at a low price. You need to check that the cost of selling the options does not outweigh the amount you will receive for them.

Buying a put option

Let's now examine the various scenarios that can arise when you purchase a put option and the alternative courses of action that are available to you under each scenario. These scenarios are essentially the same as when you buy a call option, except that you are looking for a fall in the market value of the underlying stock, not a rise. Let's begin by referring to example 6.5.

Example 6.5

Assume you believe the market price of ANZ stock will fall by $1.00 in the next month and you want to profit from this decrease in price.

Current market value of ANZ	$21.30
Date today	1 April
Put option price	$0.80
Exercise price	$21.50
Expiry month	May

In example 6.5, you have decided to buy five in-the-money put options at $0.80 each. This will cost you $400.00 (five contracts at $0.80 per share multiplied by 100 shares per contract). By purchasing these options, you now have the right to sell 500 shares in ANZ for the exercise price of $21.50. You are able to exercise this right at any time between now and the option expiry at the end of May.

There are a number of actions you may take depending on the movement in the market price of ANZ. We will examine each of these based on the following three scenarios:

⇨ The market value of ANZ increases.

⇨ The market value of ANZ does not change.

⇨ The market value of ANZ decreases.

Scenario 1: the market value of ANZ increases

In buying put options you are predicting a fall in the market value of the underlying stock. If the market value of the underlying stock increases, your option will lose value. If the market value of the underlying stock moves above the strike price of the put option, the only value in your option will be time value. This time value will decrease the further the market value of the underlying stock moves above the strike price and the closer you move to the expiry date.

Let's assume that the market price of ANZ has increased by $1.10 to $22.40 in the four weeks since you purchased your put option. This is not good news for you. Your option is now only worth $0.10. At $22.40 the market value of ANZ is now well above the strike price of your option of $21.50, so your option no longer has any intrinsic value. The time value of $0.10 will also erode as you move closer to the expiry date.

Our scenario can be now summarised in example 6.6.

Example 6.6

The market value of ANZ has increased from $21.30 to $22.40 since you purchased your put options.

Current market value of ANZ	$22.40
Date today	1 May
Expiry month	May
Put option cost	$0.80
Exercise price	$21.50
Put option current value	$0.10

As in example 6.4 where your call options failed to move in your direction, you have the same three alternative courses of action when put options fail to move in your direction.

⇨ Sell your options at a loss now.

⇨ Hold your options longer, in the expectation that the market price of ANZ will fall more than $0.10 below the strike price before the expiry date.

⇨ Let your options expire worthless.

You would not exercise your options, as this would result in selling your ANZ shares, assuming you owned them, at $21.50, $0.90 below the current market value of $22.40.

You need to decide if the market value of ANZ will move more than $0.10 below $21.50 before the expiry date. However, given the options are only worth $0.10, it is likely that your transaction costs to sell the options will exceed the cost of sale. Therefore, you would most likely hold the options in the event that they gain some intrinsic value, and if not let them expire worthless.

Scenario 2: the market value of ANZ does not change

If the market value of your underlying stock, ANZ, does not change or only changes by a small amount, the value of your put option will not increase. In fact, the value of your put option will decrease due to the reduction in time value as you near the expiry date.

As with purchasing call options when the price of the underlying stock remains steady, you have three alternative courses of action.

⇨ Exercise your options and sell your ANZ shares at the exercise price of $21.50, $0.20 above the current market value.

⇨ Sell your options.

⇨ Hold your options longer, in the expectation that the market price of ANZ will decrease and then take the first or second action in this list.

Exercise your options

If you own 500 ANZ shares and you wish to sell them, you can exercise your options and receive $21.50 per share for a total of $10 750 for your 500 shares. You will be selling your shares at just $0.20 above the market value. You would need to ensure that the $100.00 benefit of exercising your options was in excess of your transaction costs. Generally, you will be charged an exercise fee in addition to the usual brokerage fee. At the current market value, your total loss on this transaction would be as follows:

Strike price received on sale ($21.50 × 500 shares)	$10 750.00
Market price of ANZ ($21.30 × 500 shares)	($10 650.00)
Premium paid for the option	($400.00)
Net loss*	($300.00)**

* This ignores your transaction costs, which must be factored in to your analysis.

** This loss is in relation to your put option only. The total profit or loss you would realise on selling your shares would be dependent on their original cost price.

You paid $400.00 for the right to sell 300 ANZ shares at $21.50. Remember, this is a right, not an obligation, and you are not obligated to sell these shares unless you want to by exercising your put options.

Sell your options

Your second course of action is to sell your put options. Your decision to sell your options at this point in time is based on your expectation of the movement in price of the underlying stock. If you no longer believe that the underlying stock value will fall enough to cover further time decay, and do not currently own the stock and wish to sell it, then selling your options would be a reasonable course of action.

Our scenario can be now summarised as follows:

Sale price of put options ($0.30 × 5 contracts × 100 shares)	$150.00
Premium paid for the option	($400.00)
Net loss*	($250.00)

* This ignores your transaction costs, which must be factored in to your analysis.

Hold your options

Your third course of action is to hold your options. You would do this if your expectation was that the price of ANZ will fall by more than $0.30 before expiry, to offset the fall in time value of the options (currently $0.30). It is important to note that the time value of your options will decrease at a faster rate the closer you get to the expiry date.

You may also wish to hold your options longer if your reason for purchasing them was to insure against a fall in the market price of ANZ shares over the term of the options.

You would still need to take action to either exercise your options or sell your options before the expiry date if they held intrinsic value at expiry. If not, the options will expire worthless.

Scenario 3: the market value of ANZ decreases

If the market value of the underlying stock falls, the value of your put option will most likely increase. As your put option is currently in-the-money, the intrinsic value of your option will increase; however, this increase will be offset by a fall in time value. Let's say that ANZ has fallen in market value by $1.00 to $20.30 in the four weeks since you bought your put option. The market value of your put option is now $1.60. This increase of $0.80 is represented by the $1.00 increase in the intrinsic value of your option, less a decrease in the time value of $0.20. Our scenario can be now summarised in example 6.7 (overleaf).

Example 6.7

The market value of ANZ has fallen from $21.30 to $20.30 since you purchased your call options.

Current market value of ANZ	$20.30
Date today	1 May
Expiry month	May
Call option cost	$0.80
Exercise price	$21.50
Call option current value	$1.60

As outlined in example 6.2 with call options that moved in your direction, you have three courses of action.

⇨ Exercise your options and sell your ANZ shares at the exercise price of $21.50, $1.20 above the current market value.

⇨ Sell your options at a profit.

⇨ Hold your options longer, in the expectation of a further decrease in the market price of ANZ and then take the first or second action in this list.

Chapter summary

⇨ When buying call options, you will have an expectation that the market value of the underlying stock will increase over the life of your option.

⇨ When buying put options, you will have an expectation that the market value of the underlying stock will fall over the life of your option.

⇨ When buying options, you are buying a right to buy or sell the underlying stock. You do not have an obligation to do so.

⇨ Whenever you buy options, the action you take will be determined by three factors:

⊐ The movement in the price of the underlying stock.

⊐ Your reasons for buying the option.

⊐ Your risk profile and willingness to wait for price to move in your direction within a limited time frame.

⇨ There are three main scenarios that you will potentially face as an option buyer:

⊐ The market value of the underlying stock moves in your favour.

⊐ The market value of the underlying stock does not change.

⊐ The market value of the underlying stock moves against your position.

⇨ You will have a number of alternative courses of action that you can take based on the movement in market value of the underlying stock.

⇨ You have four actions available to you:

⊐ Sell your options.

⊐ Exercise your options.

⊐ Let your options expire worthless.

⊐ Hold your options closer to expiry and then either sell them, exercise them or let them expire worthless.

⇨ If your options have fallen in price and are worth very little, you need to consider your transaction costs before deciding to sell them.

chapter 7

Selling options: the scenarios

In this chapter we are going to move from buying options to selling options. Many people have more difficulty in understanding selling options as the process involves selling first and then buying later to close the position. As options are an intangible asset, not a physical asset, selling them is not as complicated as you might believe.

Selling options

When you buy an option, you are buying the right to buy or sell 100 shares of the underlying stock at the strike price, any time before the option expires. Therefore, it follows that an option seller, or option writer, is granting the right to buy or sell 100 shares of the underlying stock at the strike price, any time before the option expires. As you are selling a right, there is no asset you need to acquire first in order to do this.

As a call option seller, you are paid a premium for granting this right to the buyer. In receiving this premium, you are then obligated to deliver the underlying shares at the strike price, if the buyer exercises the option. You have no control over whether the option will be exercised or not.

When selling options, you are generally speculating that the price of the underlying stock will move insufficiently or in a direction that will result in the options decreasing in value and ultimately expiring worthless. This will allow you to retain the option premium as profit and the option will not be exercised against you.

Tip

The reduction in value due to time decay works in favour of the seller.

However, if you are wrong, you may need to close out your option at a loss or your options may be exercised. Depending upon the options you sell, your risk of loss can be significant if the market moves strongly against your position.

The actions you take after selling your options will be determined by the following factors:

⇨ the type of option you have sold

⇨ the price movement of the underlying stock and the effect this has on the option

⇨ your view on any further price movement of the underlying stock and how this will affect the value of your options

⇨ your reasons for selling the options and, for covered call options, your strategy around holding the underlying stock

⇨ your risk tolerance.

We will now take you through the scenarios you potentially face as a writer of covered call options, naked call options and put options.

Selling a covered call option

When selling a covered call option, you are selling the right to the buyer to buy the underlying stock at the strike price at any time before the option expires. You also own the underlying stock that will be delivered to the buyer if the option is exercised.

As an option seller, you have no control over whether the option will be exercised or not. This is the right of the option buyer. You do, however, have the choice of keeping your option position open and may close your option position anytime before it is exercised or expires. Once a call option is exercised it is too late to close your position. You must deliver the underlying stock to the buyer at the strike price. Let's refer to example 7.1 to illustrate this.

Example 7.1

Assume you own 300 shares in a stock priced at $25.00 and believe that the price of this stock is going to remain flat over the next few months. You decide to sell three covered calls with a strike price of $26.00 for $1.50.

Current market value of stock	$25.00
Date today	1 April
Call option premium	$1.50
Total premium received	$450.00
Exercise price	$26.00
Expiry month	June

In selling these covered calls, you now have the obligation to sell your 300 shares at $26 to the option holder if your option is exercised any time between now and the expiry date in June.

There are a number of actions that you may take in managing this open option position depending upon the movement in the market price of the underlying stock. We will have a look at each of the following four scenarios:

⇨ The market value of the stock increases but stays below the strike price.

⇨ The market value of the stock increases above the strike price.

⇨ The market value of the stock remains flat.

⇨ The market value of the stock decreases.

Scenario 1: the market value of the stock increases but stays below the strike price

Let's assume that the market value of the stock increases but remains below the strike price of $26. The option is still out-of-the-money, so it has no intrinsic value. The time value would have increased as the likelihood of the option moving into the money has increased; however, this would be offset by time decay as the option approaches the expiry date. Our scenario can be now summarised in example 7.2.

Example 7.2

In the two months since you sold your options, the underlying stock price has moved up $0.90 to $25.90.

Current market value of stock	$25.90
Exercise price	$26.00
Current option price	$0.50
Date today	1 June
Expiry month	June

You have two alternative courses of action.

⇨ Close your option position.

⇨ Hold your option position.

Close your option position

With the market price of your shares just $0.10 under the strike price, you may be feeling nervous that the options may move into the money before the expiry date. If the options move into the money, they may be exercised at any time by the buyer. If you did not wish to carry this risk, you could close your option position by buying back the options at $0.50, as you can see in the following summary.

Call option sale proceeds ($1.50 × 300.00)	$450.00
Call option cost to close ($0.50 × 300)	($150.00)
Net profit*	$300.00

* This ignores your transaction costs, which must be factored in to your analysis.

By closing your option position, you are guaranteeing that your options will not be exercised and you still realise a profit of $300 before transaction costs. However, you are giving up the opportunity to retain the full option premium if the market value of the shares stays below $26 up until the expiry date.

Hold your option position

If the market value of the underlying stock remains below the strike price of $26, the options will continue to suffer time decay and expire worthless. You do not need to take any immediate action when the stock price is still below the strike price.

However, you should monitor the position closely, particularly if you wish to retain the underlying stock and want to avoid exercise of the options.

Scenario 2: the market value of the stock increases above the strike price

Let's assume that the market value of the stock increases above the strike price of $26. The option is now in-the-money and will have intrinsic value. You now have a decision to make as you are at risk of your option being exercised. Our scenario can be summarised in example 7.3.

Example 7.3

In the two months since you sold your options, the underlying stock price has moved up $1.50 to $26.50.

Current market value of stock	$26.50
Exercise price	$26.00
Current option price	$1.00
Date today	1 June
Expiry month	June

You have two alternative courses of action.

⇨ Close your option position.

⇨ Hold your option position.

Close your option position

As your options are now in-the-money, if you do not wish to have them exercised you can close your position by buying back the options. As you received $1.50 in premium for your options, you will break even or make a slight profit (before transaction costs) if you buy the call options back for anything up to $1.50 per option.

If the value of the option moves above $1.50 per option, you will make a loss on your options by closing out the position. However, this will be offset by the increase in value of your underlying shares, as you can see in example 7.4.

Example 7.4

The market value of your shares moves up sharply to $28.00 per share. You do not wish to sell your shares at the strike price of $26.00, so you decide to quickly close your option position to avoid exercise. The options are now priced at $2.75, being $2.00 of intrinsic value and $0.75 of remaining time value.

Call option sale proceeds ($1.50 × 300)	$450.00
Call option cost to close ($2.75 × 300)	($825.00)
Net loss on options*	($375.00)
Value of shares when options sold	$7 500.00
Market value of shares (300 × $28.00)	$8 400.00
Unrealised gain on shares	$900.00

* This ignores your transaction costs, which must be factored in to your analysis.

By closing your option position in example 7.4, you are guaranteeing that your options will not be exercised and you can keep your shares. The options have cost you $375 before transaction costs. However, this cost is offset by the unrealised gain you make on your shares of $900.

Hold your option position
You may be quite happy to have your options exercised and sell them at the strike price of $26, as, for example, this may have been your target price for your share strategy. If your options are exercised, which is most likely, you will retain your option premium and realise a gain on the sale of your shares.

The downside is that you are missing out on the additional gain you would have made if you could sell your shares at the current market price, as this is now higher than the strike price of your call options. This is simply an opportunity cost and not a realised loss.

Scenario 3: the market value of the stock remains flat

Let's assume that the market value of the stock remains steady and trades in a price range of $24.80 to $25.30. The option is out-of-the-money and has no intrinsic value. Your options will have fallen in value due to time decay as you approach the expiry date. You have two alternative courses of action.

Close your option position

Your options are still out-of-the-money and time decay has seen the value of the options fall to $0.50. This is good news for you as an option seller. Unless the market price of the shares moves up significantly to over $26 in the few weeks to expiry, the options will expire worthless and you will retain the option premium of $450.

You would only consider closing your option position if you believed that the shares were going to have an unexpected and sharp increase in price to push your options into the money and you do not wish to be exposed to the risk of exercise.

Hold your option position

In the absence of any belief that the share price will move up over $26 to push the options into the money before expiry, your best course of action is to hold your options.

If the market value of underlying shares remains below the strike price, this is a good outcome for a seller of covered call options. The value of your shares has remained steady, plus you retained the total option premium as profit.

Scenario 4: the market value of the stock decreases

Let's assume that the market value of the stock falls. This is good news for your option position, but bad news for your stock position. A falling stock price will mean that your options will remain out-of-the-money and you will retain the option premium. However, the falling stock price also means that you lose value in your stock position. Our scenario can be summarised in example 7.5.

Example 7.5

In the two months since you sold your options, the underlying stock price has fallen to $24.00.

Call option sale proceeds ($1.50 × 300)	$450.00
Current option value	$0.20
Current market value of shares	$7 200.00
Unrealised loss on your shares	($300.00)
Date today	1 June
Expiry month	June

Once again, you have two alternative courses of action.

⇨ Close your option position.

⇨ Hold your option position.

Close your option position

Your decision to close your option position will depend upon your view of any further price movement in the underlying shares. If you feel that the stock will continue to fall and you wish to sell your shares now, you will need to close your option position first. As you have sold covered call options, you are unable to sell the underlying stock that is 'covering' your option position until you close it.

To close your option position, you would simply need to buy back the options at their current market value. You may also consider other alternatives to protecting your share position, such as buying put options.

Hold your option position

As you sold the covered call options for $1.50, they have provided you with protection against a fall in your underlying shares of up to $1.50. The premium from your covered call options will offset the loss on your underlying shares, as we summarise in example 7.6.

Example 7.6

In the two months since you sold your options, the underlying stock price has fallen to $24.00.

Call option sale proceeds ($1.50 × 300)	$450.00
Current market value of shares	$7 200.00
Unrealised loss on your shares	($300.00)
Net position on your options and shares*	$150.00

* Net position does not take into account transaction costs.

In example 7.6, the $1.00 fall in the value of your shares has been offset by the $1.50 premium you received on selling your options. If the value of the stock fell below $23.50, or more than $1.50, you would move into a net loss position.

Selling a naked call option

When selling a naked call option, you are selling the right to the buyer to buy the underlying stock at the strike price at any time before the option expires. However, you do not own the underlying stock. This is a high risk strategy that can result in significant losses for the option seller.

If your naked call option is exercised, your obligation is to deliver the underlying stock to the buyer. In theory, this would require you to purchase the stock at the current market price and then sell this stock to the buyer at the strike price of the option. In practice, ASX Clear undertakes these transactions and you are simply required to pay the difference in price plus transaction fees. This exposes you to unlimited risk, as there is no theoretical limit on how high the stock price might go.

The scenarios that might arise, and your courses of action, are the same as for covered calls. There are, however, two key factors that will influence how you manage the two different types of call option positions. These are your risk tolerance and margin requirements.

Your risk tolerance

When selling covered call options, if the market moves against you and your options are exercised, you simply have to sell your shares at the strike price. Although you miss out on potential profit on the shares, you do not incur a realised loss on the shares due to the sale. The loss is not directly taken from your trading account.

When selling naked call options, you must pay for any loss incurred on the exercise of the options. And you have no control over the size or timing of this loss other than closing out your position.

As a result, your decision to hold a naked call option position that is near or in-the-money will be influenced by your risk tolerance. Your exposure to the potential for unlimited risk is likely to change the way in which you manage a naked call option compared with a covered call option. It does not change the choices available to you — but it will change which choices you make and when you make them.

Margin requirements

As a seller of options, you are required to lodge security as margin for your open option positions. The level of margin increases as the value of the options increase. When you sell covered calls, your margin is covered by your underlying shares. If the market value of the shares increases significantly and you have a large loss on your options, you are still not required to lodge any further margin.

When selling naked call options, as the market value of the underlying stock moves deeper into the money, you will be required to lodge additional margin to cover the additional risk. A margin call may influence your decision to continue holding your option position. In addition, if you are unable to or fail to meet your margin call, your broker may close your position, and/or sell some of your existing securities to cover it.

Selling a put option

When selling a put option, you are granting the right to the buyer to sell 100 shares of the underlying stock to you at the strike price any time before expiry. As the market price of the underlying stock rises, the value of the put option falls. This is advantageous to the put option seller. However, as the market price of the underlying stock falls, the value of the put option rises, which exposes the put option seller to potential losses.

Your risk when selling a put option is that the market value of the underlying stock will fall below the strike price, and if the option is exercised, you will be required to buy that stock at the strike price (above its market value). Your risk of loss is therefore, in theory, only limited by the strike price of the option and could be significant.

We will now look at the scenarios that can arise if you sell a put option. We will use example 7.7 to illustrate this.

Example 7.7

You believe the market price of ANZ stock will increase from its current market value of $21.30 in the next two months and at worst will not fall below $20.50. You decide to sell 40 put options with a strike price of $20.50 for $0.50.

Current market value of ANZ	$21.30
Exercise price	$20.50
Put option price	$0.50
Proceeds from selling put options	$2 000.00

In example 7.7 you have sold out-of-the-money put options and you are speculating that they will remain out-of-the-money until the expiry date of the options.

There are a number of actions that you might take depending on the movement in the market price of ANZ. We will discuss these based on the following four scenarios:

⇨ The market value of the stock falls but stays above the strike price.

⇨ The market value of the stock falls below the strike price.

⇨ The market value of the stock remains flat.

⇨ The market value of the stock increases.

Scenario 1: the market value of the stock falls but stays above the strike price

Let's assume that the market value of ANZ falls but stays above the strike price of $20.50. The options are still out-of-the-money, so they have no intrinsic value. The time value would increase as the likelihood of the option moving into the money has increased; however, this would be offset by time decay as the option approaches the expiry date. You have two alternative courses of action.

⇨ Close your option position.

⇨ Hold your option position.

If your options remain out-of-the-money, you will not be required to fulfil any obligations and they will expire worthless. You will retain the option premium. If you believed that the market value of ANZ will remain above the strike price of your options until expiry, then holding your position is a reasonable course of action.

However, you should monitor the position closely, particularly due to the risks involved in light of a sudden fall in the price of the underlying stock.

If, however, you are feeling nervous that the options may move into the money before the expiry date, you might consider closing your position early. You are exposed to a significant risk of loss if the market value of the underlying shares has a large sudden fall in price. For every dollar that ANZ falls below $20.50, your put options will increase in value by $1.00, costing you $4000.00 per $1.00 fall. If you did not wish to carry the risk of a sudden price fall putting your options in-the-money, you could close your option position by buying back the options.

By closing your option position before expiry and while it remains out-of-the-money, you are guaranteeing that your options will not be exercised. However, you are giving up the opportunity to retain the full option premium if the market value of the shares stays above $20.50 up until the expiry date.

Scenario 2: the market value of the stock falls below the strike price

Let's assume that the market value of the stock falls below the strike price of $20.50. The option is now in-the-money and will have intrinsic value. As revealed in example 7.8, you now have a decision to make as you are at risk of your option being exercised.

Example 7.8

In the two months since you sold your options, the market price of ANZ has plummeted on some bad news and fallen $2.50 to $18.80.

Current market value of stock	$18.80
Exercise price	$20.50
Current option price	$1.90

You have two alternative courses of action.

⇨ Close your option position.

⇨ Hold your option position.

Close your option position

As your put options are now in-the-money, if you do not wish to have them exercised, you can close your position by buying back the options. As you received $0.50 in premium for your options, this will offset some of the cost of buying back the put options. However, as the put options are now valued at $1.90, you will make a loss on this transaction. This is illustrated in example 7.9.

Example 7.9	
Current market value of stock	$18.80
Exercise price	$20.50
Current put option price	$1.90
Put option sale proceeds ($0.50 × 4000)	$2 000.00
Put option cost to close ($1.90 × 4000)	($7 600.00)
Net loss*	($5 600.00)

* This ignores your transaction costs, which must be factored in to your analysis.

By closing your option position, you are limiting your loss on the transaction in light of the possibility of a further fall in the price of the underlying shares. The option has cost you $5600 before transaction costs.

Example 7.9 illustrates the risks involved in selling put options. A sharp fall in the value of the underlying shares can create significant losses for the put option writer.

Hold your option position

You may feel that the sudden fall in price is temporary or the shares will not fall any further during the remaining life of the option. In this case, you may wish to risk exercise of the options in the hope that the share price will return quickly to its previous levels and reduce your loss. If the price of the shares remains below $20.50, it is most likely that the options will be exercised and you will need to buy 4000 shares in ANZ at the strike price of $20.50.

If the value of ANZ continues to fall, your losses will continue to increase. This loss is potentially only limited to the strike price of the underlying stock if the market value of ANZ fell to zero (although unlikely). In this example, every $1 fall in the value of ANZ below $20.50 costs you $4000.00 up to a potential total of $82 000.00.

Scenario 3: the market value of the stock remains flat

Let's assume that the market value of ANZ remains steady and trades in a price range of $21.00 to $21.50. Your put option is out-of-the-money and has no intrinsic value. Your put options will have fallen in value due to time decay as you approach the expiry date.

This is good news for you as the writer of put options. If the market price of ANZ stays above $20.50 up until the expiry date, the options will expire worthless and you will retain the option premium of $2000.00.

You can choose to hold your position to expiry or close your position early.

You would only consider closing your option position if you believed that the shares were going to have an unexpected and sharp fall in price to push your options into the money and you do not wish to be exposed to the risk of loss.

Scenario 4: the market value of the stock increases

Let's assume that the market value of ANZ moves up $1.00 to $22.30. This is good news for anyone selling put options. A rising stock price will mean that your options will remain out-of-the-money and you will retain the option premium if you hold them to expiry.

Chapter summary

⇨ When selling options, you are granting the right to buy or sell 100 shares of the underlying stock at the strike price, any time before the option expires.

⇨ As an option seller, you have no control over whether your option is exercised. This is the right of the buyer.

⇨ When you sell options, you receive the option premium first.

⇨ You can close your option position at any time by purchasing the option before it is exercised.

⇨ Once an option is exercised, you cannot close the position.

⇨ Whenever you sell options, the action you take will be determined by the following factors:

  ⌶ The type of option you have sold.

  ⌶ The direction and range of movement in price of the underlying stock.

  ⌶ Your view on the movement in price of the underlying stock to expiry.

  ⌶ Your reasons for selling the options and, for covered call options, your strategy around holding the underlying stock.

  ⌶ Your risk tolerance.

⇨ Selling covered call options is a conservative strategy with limited loss, but an unlimited opportunity cost.

⇨ Selling naked call options or put options are high risk strategies that carry the risk of significant losses.

⇨ There are four main scenarios that you will potentially face as an option writer:

  ⋈ The market value of the underlying stock moves against you but the option remains out-of-the-money.

  ⋈ The market value of the underlying stock moves against you and the option moves into the money.

  ⋈ The market value of the underlying stock remains flat.

  ⋈ The market value of the underlying stock moves in your favour.

⇨ You have two actions available to you in managing your option position:

  ⋈ Sell your options.

  ⋈ Hold your options closer to expiry and then either sell them or let them expire worthless.

⇨ If your option is exercised, your only course of action is to meet your obligations under the option.

chapter 8

Choosing your option strategy

In this chapter we will look at the key factors you need to consider when choosing an option strategy. When trading shares, you really have the choice to buy, then sell or hold your position. With options there are many more choices, each with different risks and opportunities.

Regardless of the strategy you choose, your objective will be to either make a profit, or limit a potential loss. In pursuit of these aims, as a buyer of options you seek to purchase your option at the lowest price possible, and then sell it (or exercise it) at the highest price possible. As an option writer, you work directly against the buyers in seeking to sell your options at the highest price possible, and then close them out at the lowest price possible or see them expire worthless.

For any option trade, the movement in the option premium while you hold it will determine if you make a profit or loss. You therefore must consider all the factors that will cause a change in your option premium.

These factors include:

⇨ movement in the price of the underlying stock (and all the factors that may affect this)

⇨ time to expiry and time decay

⇨ changes in volatility.

This is in contrast to share trading, where you only need to consider the movement in the price of the stock. Time decay and changes in volatility are unique to trading in options. Although the movement in the price of the underlying stock is the most significant factor affecting most options, it is important to consider the impact of time decay and any changes in volatility of the underlying stock price when crafting your option trading strategy.

Tip

Even if the price of the underlying stock moves in your direction, you can still make a loss due to the impact of time decay or an unexpected change in volatility.

Movement in price

The most significant factor affecting the price of your option is movements in price of the underlying stock. So you need to have formed a view on how the market price of the underlying stock is going to move. Due to the time limitations in trading options, you also need to form a view of the price movement of the underlying stock over a specific time period, and match your option expiry to this time frame.

You can determine your view on the price movement of the underlying stock using fundamental analysis, technical analysis or a combination of both. The approach used to form your view is not relevant to choosing your option strategy, as long as you are able to speculate about the movement of price within the limited life of an option.

The following general guidelines can be used in relation to choosing an option strategy based on your view of the price movement in the underlying stock:

⇨ If you are expecting significant movement in the market price of the underlying stock, buying options may be a suitable strategy.

⇨ If you are not expecting a significant movement in the market price of the underlying stock, writing options may be a suitable strategy.

The reason for this is the impact of time decay. For an option buyer, any positive movement in the market price of the underlying stock needs to be large enough to offset the time decay experienced while holding the option. The movement in the market price of the underlying stock needs to be large enough to put the option in-the-money (if it is not there already), and increase intrinsic value enough to offset the reduction in time value.

If you are expecting that the price of the underlying stock will remain within a limited price range, you may consider writing options as a strategy. The reason for this is once again time decay. If the underlying stock price remains fairly static, there will be little change in the intrinsic value and a decrease in time value, causing the price of the option to fall. The profit potential for an option writer is always the premium received, so large price movements in their favour are not advantageous to option writers as they do not affect the profit made.

Tip

Option writers are generally looking for time decay to reduce the value of the options they write so that their options expire worthless. The option writer then retains the option premium as a profit.

Time decay

All options have a limited life that is defined by the option expiry date. All options will be subject to time decay over the life of the option and this reduction in time value will increase as the option approaches the expiry date.

Time works against option buyers as they are speculating on a significant price movement in the underlying stock to occur before the expiry date. Not only do option buyers need to speculate on a price movement, this movement must occur before the expiry date.

Tip

Your view on the timing of price movement in the underlying stock will influence your choice of expiry month.

Time decay also works against option buyers, as it reduces the value of an option despite any other favourable movements in the price of the underlying stock. Any increase in the intrinsic value of an option will always be reduced by the time decay of the option.

As an option buyer selecting an expiry month, you need to balance against having enough time for the stock price to move in your favour and the cost of this time. Longer dated options have a higher time value and as a result will also have a higher premium. The success of your option strategy will be highly dependent upon the time that you have to option expiry date, and the amount you paid for that time.

As an option seller, you need to balance the additional premium you receive for a longer dated option against the increased possibility that the underlying stock price will move against you in this time and you will incur losses over and above your option premium.

Volatility

Volatility is the price range in which the underlying stock is expected to move. As we discussed in chapter 4 on pricing, volatility of the underlying stock is a key factor determining the time value of an option. If there is a significant change in volatility in the underlying stock, this will affect the time value and thus the premium price of an option.

If the volatility of the underlying stock reduces, this means that the price range in which the stock will move has been reduced. It then follows that the time value of the option will reduce as the stock is less likely to achieve a price movement that will result in a profit for the option buyer.

On the other hand, if you have an unexpected increase in the volatility of the underlying stock price, this will increase the time value of the options. In example 8.1, we discuss the impact of a change in volatility on option price.

Example 8.1

You have been watching the price of a mining stock for some time. It has been moving within a limited range in the last few months and has been experiencing reduced volatility recently. You feel that the stock is about to break out into a trending upward move, which will create a significant increase to the volatility of the stock price.

In considering buying options over this stock, you need take into consideration your view of both an increase in the price of the stock and an increase in the volatility of the stock price.

The movement in the stock price will affect the price of the option. The impact of this movement on your option price will depend on the type of option you buy and the current market value of the stock in relation to the strike price of the option (that is, if it is in-the-money).

The change in volatility of the underlying stock price will cause an increase to the option premium, if this change has not been anticipated by the market and priced into the option already.

If you determine that a stock price will experience an increase in price volatility, a strategy involving buying options is likely to be beneficial as this will result in an increase in time value of your option. However, if you determine that a stock price will experience a reduction in volatility, this will benefit an option writer by reducing the value of the option.

Chapter summary

⇨ Your objective in trading options is to either produce a profit or minimise a potential loss.

⇨ As an option buyer, you want to purchase options at the lowest price and sell them at the highest price.

⇨ As an option seller, you want to sell options at the highest price and either close them at a low price or see them expire worthless.

⇨ It is the movement in the option premium that determines the success of your option strategy.

⇨ Your choice of option strategy will be influenced by three main factors:

　　⌂ Your view of the movement in price of the underlying stock.

　　⌂ Time to expiry and time decay.

　　⌂ Your view on the volatility of the underlying stock price.

⇨ The most significant factor affecting the price of an option is movement in price of the underlying stock.

⇨ A significant movement in the price of the underlying stock will favour option buying strategies.

⇨ A small or flat movement in the price of the underlying stock will favour option writing strategies.

⇨ Time works against option buyers, as they must achieve a significant price movement within the limited life of an option. This price movement must also offset the impact of time decay on an option.

⇨ Your view on the timing of price movement in the underlying stock will influence your choice of expiry month.

⇨ A longer dated option will be more expensive than a shorter dated option as it will have a higher time value in the option premium.

⇨ Your option strategy must take into account both the benefits and costs associated with a particular expiry month.

⇨ Any changes in volatility will affect the value of an option.

⇨ Unexpected increases in volatility of the underlying stock price will increase the time value and as such the premium price of an option.

chapter 9

Strategies for buying call options

In this chapter we will discuss some general attributes, benefits and risks specifically involved in strategies for buying call options. Generally, buyers of call options have a bullish view about the market price of a specific stock, and are looking to profit from this expected increase in market value.

The most well-known strategy for buying call options is speculating on an increase in the market value of the underlying stock. It is a basic strategy that is more popular than buying put options, as it is more easily understood. In this chapter we look at the speculative strategy as well as a number of other less well-known strategies involving buying call options.

Buying call options

When buying call options, you are speculating that the price of the underlying stock will increase by a significant amount within a limited time period in order to produce a profit. If you are proven correct, the percentage returns on your trade are immense. However, if you are wrong, you will lose some or all of the initial premium you paid.

You are buying the right to purchase 100 shares of the underlying stock at the strike price at any time before the expiry date. You pay a premium for this right. Once you have purchased your option, you have three alternatives:

⇨ Sell your option before expiry.

⇨ Exercise your option before expiry.

⇨ Allow the option to expire worthless.

As we outlined in chapter 6, the action you take will depend upon the movement in the market price of the underlying share, your expectation of any future movement before expiry, your reasons for buying the call and your risk tolerance.

Time is a significant factor in determining how you manage your option trade. Every day that you hold an option, the time value of your option will decrease. And it will decrease at an increasing rate as you approach the expiry date. In fact, even if the market price of the underlying stock increases before expiry, you may still lose money on your option due to the effect of time decay cancelling out any increase in intrinsic value.

Tip

The biggest problem for call option buyers is lack of time and declining time value in their options.

Often the market value of the underlying stock will increase over the life of the option, but it may not increase by enough to offset the decline in time value. As a result, the call option buyer does not earn a profit on their investment. This scenario is examined in example 9.1.

Example 9.1

You decided to purchase a $40.00 WPL call option for $3.50 when the market price of WPL was $40.00.

By the expiry date, the price of WPL had risen to $42.00; however, your call option was now only worth $2.00.

How can you have lost money on your option when the market price of the underlying stock has risen?

When you purchased your option, it was at-the-money. As a result, the total option premium of $3.50 consisted of time value. So even though the stock price increased by $2.00 and the intrinsic value of your option increased by $2.00, this was offset by time decay of $3.50.

Increase in intrinsic value	$2.00
Decrease in time value	($3.50)
Your net loss on the option*	($1.50)

* This calculation does not include transaction costs.

You can see from example 9.1 that in order to make a profit on buying a call option the market value of the underlying stock needs to increase by enough to both:

⇨ offset the time decay

⇨ create growth in the intrinsic value of the option.

There are several reasons why you might consider buying call options as your trading strategy. These include the following:

⇨ gain leverage

⇨ limit your risk

⇨ delay a stock purchase

⇨ speculate for profit.

Strategy 1: gain leverage

Buying call options provides you with the benefit of leverage. You only need to provide a fraction of the capital to buy call options compared with purchasing the stock outright. This allows you to magnify your percentage returns if you are proven correct. We examine this in example 9.2.

Example 9.2

You are speculating that there will be a large increase in the market price of CSL in the next two months. You decided to purchase 30 $32.00 CSL call options for $1.50 when the market price of CSL was $32.00.

Two months later, your prediction has proven correct and the price of CSL has increased by $2.75 to $34.75. Your call option is now worth $3.00.

Comparing the return on your investment with buying the shares directly, we have the following results.

	Options	*Shares*
Initial investment	30 options	3 000 shares
Unit cost	$1.50	$32.00
Cost	$4 500.00	$96 000.00
Sale price	$9 000.00	$104 250.00
Net profit*	$4 500.00	$8 250.00
Return on investment cost*	100%	8.5%

* Net profit does not account for transaction costs.

As you can see from example 9.2, the percentage returns are magnified when trading options over shares due to the advantage of leverage. In this example, the dollar profit was lower on your options due to the lost time value (your purchase price was all time value as the options were bought at-the-money); however, the percentage return is much higher due to the lower initial investment cost. An 8.5 per cent rise in the stock price has produced a 100 per cent increase in the value of your call option.

Strategy 2: limit your risk

Purchasing call options, as opposed to purchasing the stock directly, also allows you to limit your losses if the stock price falls. You may wish to speculate on an increase in the market value of a particular stock; however, you may also not wish to be exposed to potential losses if the market value falls significantly. If you purchase the stock, you are exposed to the full amount of any fall in the stock price. With call options, however, you can only ever lose the premium you paid, regardless of how far the stock price might fall. This scenario is revealed in example 9.3.

Example 9.3

You are speculating that there will be an increase in the market price of CSL in the next two months. You decided to purchase 30 $33.50 CSL call options for $0.50 when the market price of CSL was $32.00.

Unfortunately, two months later on option expiry the price of CSL has actually fallen by $1.50 to $30.50. Your call option is now worthless.

Comparing the return on your investment with buying the shares directly, we have the following results.

	Options	*Shares*
Initial investment	30 options	3 000 shares
Unit cost	$0.50	$32.00
Cost	$1 500.00	$96 000.00
Sale price	$0.00	$91 500.00
Net loss*	($1 500.00)	($4 500.00)
Percentage loss*	(100%)	(5%)

* Net profit does not account for transaction costs.

As you can see from example 9.3, even though the market value of CSL fell by $1.50, as an option buyer your loss is always limited to the premium you paid for the option, which in this example was $0.50.

Example 9.3 also shows the effect of leverage in reverse. A 5 per cent fall in the price of the underlying stock has resulted in a 100 per cent fall in the value of your call option.

Strategy 3: delay a stock purchase

When you buy a call option, you are purchasing the right to buy 100 shares of the underlying stock at the strike price anytime on or before the expiry date. Thus, you are locking in the price you will pay for the shares if you decide to exercise the option and purchase the stock before the expiry date of the option.

You may wish to invest longer term in a particular stock as you feel it will increase in value; however, for some reason you wish to delay your purchase. Or perhaps you wish to buy the stock but would like to see it increase in value first to confirm your analysis of an expected price increase. Buying a call option allows you to delay your purchase but still lock in the price at which you will purchase the stock. This scenario is outlined in example 9.4.

Example 9.4

The market has experienced some significant falls in value recently, and you wish to take advantage of the depressed prices. There is one stock you have been watching that, prior to the fall, was trading over $30 per share and is now trading at just $18 per share. You believe that the price will rebound; however, you do not have the funds available at this time.

You decide to buy a $19 call option that has five months to expiry. The premium is $1. This purchase gives you the option to purchase the stock at $19 per share any time in the next five months. You have five months to raise the funds to buy the shares and still purchase them at $19. Based on what the stock price does over this time, you can decide to sell your call options or exercise your call options and purchase the stock at $19.

Strategy 4: speculate for profit

A popular reason for buying call options is speculating to generate a short-term profit. You are simply speculating on the price of the underlying stock rising by a sufficient amount to generate a profit on your options. You are not purchasing the call options with any intention to exercise them.

Time decay will cause the value of the call option to fall as long as you are holding the option. For this reason, you need to be careful how you select the call options you wish to trade. You will need to balance the time you need for the stock to move in your direction against the time value (cost) in the option premium.

You also need to consider the strike price in relation to the current market value of the underlying stock. You need your options to be in-the-money to create an increase in intrinsic value. Call options will be cheaper when they are out-of-the-money, as a larger price movement is required to generate intrinsic value in the option.

Conditions you should look for in selecting a call option for speculation include:

⇨ The strike price should be close to the current market value of the stock. This will ensure that the increase in the underlying stock price will be reflected in the price of your option when they are in-the-money options.

⇨ The time to expiry must be long enough for your stock price to increase sufficiently to offset the time decay and generate a profit on your call options.

⇨ Options with low time value in the premium will reduce the time decay your options will incur. As time value is the value of the possibility of your option producing a profit, call options will have a low time value if the market perception is that the underlying stock price will remain stable or decrease.

Example 9.5 illustrates how speculating for profit can be used as a strategy.

Example 9.5

You have been watching a mining stock recently whose share price has been quite flat for some time at around $25.00. Based on your analysis, you believe the stock price is about to break out of its current price range and move sharply upward by at least $4.00 within a few weeks.

You decide to purchase 40 $26.00 call options for $0.10. These call options are inexpensive as they are out-of-the-money and the market expectation for the stock is to remain flat. You only wish to risk a small amount in order to be able to take advantage of this potential move.

If the stock does not increase above $26.10, then you will have lost the premium you paid of $400.00.

However, if the stock price does increase to $29.00 as you expect, you will make a profit of $15 600.00.

Risks and disadvantages of buying call options

There are some risks and disadvantages to purchasing call options that you need to be aware of. Three main risks you need to consider are time to expiry, time decay and a fall in volatility of the underlying stock price.

Time to expiry

You are playing against time. The value of the underlying stock needs to increase by a sufficient amount before the expiry date for you to make a profit on buying call options. Your risk is that the underlying stock will not move in your favour before the expiry date and you will lose some or all of your option premium.

Time decay

You also lose time value on your options for every day that you hold them. The rate at which you lose time value also increases the closer you move towards the expiry date. So you need a larger rise in the price of the underlying stock to offset the time decay the closer you get to the expiry date. This needs to be factored in to any decision to continue holding your options as you approach the expiry date.

> ### Tip
>
> *You may be correct in speculating on a price rise; however, you may not make a profit on your options if this rise is not large enough or doesn't occur before the expiry date of your options.*

It is important for you to understand the pricing of the underlying stock and how this will affect the value of your option at expiry. In particular, you need to be aware of the strike price and when your option will be in-the-money so that it has some intrinsic value. You should also know the price that the underlying stock needs to reach for you to recover the option premium you paid and break even on your trade. This will enable you to analyse the price movement required before expiry for any call options you are considering to purchase. You can then determine which strike price and expiry date is most appropriate for your call option strategy.

> ### Tip
>
> *A pay-off diagram is a great tool for you to readily see the price that the underlying stock must reach for you to offset the time decay over the life of the option.*

Fall in volatility of the underlying stock price

As we discussed in chapter 4, the time value of your call option is based upon the implied volatility of the underlying stock price. If the underlying stock price experiences a decrease in volatility, this will result in a decrease in the value of your option. The reason for this is that when the underlying stock price is experiencing a smaller range of movement, the potential to profit on your call options is reduced.

Selecting your call option

Once you have decided on your call option strategy and the underlying stock, you need to select which call option you wish to buy. There will be a range of options available with different strike prices, different premiums and different expiry dates.

So how do you choose which is the best call option to buy? The factors you need to consider in selecting your option include the:

⇨ strike price in relation to the current market value

⇨ expiry date

⇨ volatility of the underlying stock price

⇨ option premium.

Strike price in relation to the current market value

Where the strike price is in relation to the current market value of the underlying stock will determine how far the underlying stock price needs to increase to create some intrinsic value (be at-the-money), and then how far above this price you will break even and start to make a profit.

Depending upon your view of the underlying stock, you need to select a call option with a strike price that meets three conditions. You believe that the market value of the underlying stock will:

⇨ increase above the strike price so that your option has intrinsic value (unless you buy an in-the-money option)

⇨ increase sufficiently above the at-the-money value to offset the premium you paid for the option

⇨ increase even further to create enough return on your investment.

Expiry date

The expiry date is a key determinant of whether your option strategy is successful. You need the market value of the stock to meet the above three conditions before the option expires. Assessing the time frame in which a stock will move must be based on your own analysis of the stock and is often a difficult assessment.

Volatility of the underlying stock price

The volatility of the underlying stock price will determine if the price of this stock will move sufficiently within your time frame to generate a profit on your call option. A stock with low volatility experiences only a small change in price, and will be unlikely to produce a profit for a call option buyer unless the volatility increases.

Option premium

The cost of your option, or the option premium, will directly affect the profit or loss you make on your option trade. The factors affecting your option premium were discussed in chapter 4.

Some general guidelines you can use in selecting your option are as follows:

⇨ A call option with a lower strike price will:

  ¤ require a smaller increase in the share price to generate a profit

- ¤ be more expensive than a similar dated option with a higher strike price.

⇨ A call option with a longer expiry date will:

- ¤ give you a greater chance of achieving a profit on your call option as you have more time for the underlying stock price to move sufficiently in your favour

- ¤ be more expensive than a call option with a shorter expiry date.

⇨ Buying an out-of-the-money call option is consistent with a very bullish view of the underlying stock as you need a large increase in price to generate a profit on your call option.

⇨ Buying an at-the-money or an in-the-money call option is a less bullish view, but still requires an increase in value of the underlying stock price above the time value in the call option.

Your challenge in selecting a call option is to:

⇨ determine how far you believe the underlying stock price will increase

⇨ determine how long you think it will take to increase to that price

⇨ find call options that have a strike price and expiry date that fit with your analysis

⇨ calculate your break-even point based on premiums available

⇨ find the least expensive option that meets your criteria above and will generate a sufficient return on investment.

Chapter summary

⇨ When buying call options, you are speculating on an increase in price of the underlying stock.

⇨ Buying call options is a popular strategy as it is easily understood and in line with buying stocks for growth.

⇨ If your call option strategy is successful, your percentage returns can be immense.

⇨ Your risk in buying call options is limited to the premium you pay for the call option.

⇨ Time is a significant factor in a call option strategy due to the impact of time decay on the value of your option and the need for the underlying stock price to increase sufficiently before the expiry date.

⇨ There are several reasons why you might consider buying call options as your trading strategy. These include the following:

  ♯ gain leverage

  ♯ limit your risk

  ♯ delay a stock purchase

  ♯ speculate for profit.

⇨ Buying call options provides you with leverage compared with investing in the underlying stock directly.

⇨ Buying call options can limit your risk as your loss is always limited to the premium you paid for the call options. When buying the stock directly, you are exposed to all falls in value, however severe.

⇨ Buying call options can enable you to delay a planned purchase of the underlying stock but set the price now.

⇨ You can buy call options as a strategy to simply speculate on generating a short-term profit on your option trade.

⇨ The biggest disadvantage to call option buyers is time. Any strategy involving buying call options must be successful before the expiry date of the option.

⇨ Call option buyers must also account for time decay in their option strategy.

⇨ In selecting your option, you need to ensure the key components of strike price and expiry date match your strategy.

⇨ You want to buy the option that has the most advantageous strike price and expiry date and the lowest option premium.

chapter 10

Strategies for buying put options

In this chapter we are moving from a bullish view of the market to a bearish view and will focus on how you can use put options to profit from a falling stock price. As buying put options provides you with the right to sell your stock at a set price, you are able to lock in a sell price in a falling market to either profit from this move or protect existing positions.

The conventional approach to investing in stock markets is to buy in a rising market and to stay out of a falling market. Put options, however, give you an opportunity to profit from a falling market. The value of an in-the-money put option increases as the price of the underlying stock falls. The further the market falls, the more your put option increases in value.

Buying put options can also help you to protect profits in your existing stock holdings. You can lock in a sell price (strike price on your put option) so that if the value of your stock falls, it will be offset by an increase in value of your put option. This is like buying insurance for your stocks against a price drop. If the price doesn't fall, all you lose is the put option premium you paid.

Buying put options

Buying a put option gives you the right to sell a stock at the strike price any time before it expires. Even if the market price of the underlying stock has fallen below the strike price, if you exercise your put option, you are able to sell your stock at the higher strike price.

Buying put options is a strategy you can use if you are expecting a fall in market prices. As with all options, you pay a premium for your put options. If the underlying stock price does not fall, you will lose some or all of the premium you paid for the put options.

It is not necessary for you to own the underlying stock to buy put options. You are still able to profit from a falling market by simply buying and selling the put options. Remember, as a buyer, you have the right to sell the underlying stock, not the obligation to sell.

There are three alternative courses of action you can take after purchasing put options.

⇨ Sell your option before it expires.

⇨ Exercise your option before it expires.

⇨ Allow the option to expire worthless.

As we discussed in chapter 6, the course of action you take will depend upon the reasons you purchased the put options, the movement in price of the underlying stock, your expectations of any further movements in this price and your risk tolerance. If you do not own the underlying stock, your alternatives are limited to selling your option or allowing it to expire worthless.

Tip

You do not need to own the underlying stock in order to buy put options.

Time is a significant factor when buying put options, just as it is when buying call options. When buying a put option to generate a profit, you need to consider the limitations of time to expiry and time decay.

Even if the market value of the underlying stock falls over the life of a put option, if this fall is not significant enough to cover the loss of time value, you will not profit from your investment.

There are four main reasons for buying put options:

⇨ gain leverage

⇨ limit your risk

⇨ protect your existing long position

⇨ speculate for profit.

These strategies work in the same way for call options (as explained in chapter 9) except that the value of your put options increases as the market value of the underlying stock falls below the strike price of the option. Therefore, in this chapter we will only cover the points that are specifically relevant for put options under each strategy.

Strategy 1: gain leverage

Buying put options to profit from a falling share price is as simple as buying call options. You have limited risk and have the benefit of leverage compared with short selling the stock.

Short selling is a method of selling a stock on the market and then buying it back later. This is a strategy used to profit from a falling market as you sell now at the current market price, with the expectation of buying the stock back later at a lower price. There are significant restrictions on short selling shares imposed by both the stock exchange and brokers, plus not all brokers offer this service to all investors.

Short selling is essentially the opposite transaction to buying shares directly as you sell the shares first, and then buy them back at a later date. Your aim is to profit from a fall in the share price. Let's look at this process in figures 10.1 and 10.2 (overleaf).

Figure 10.1: short selling

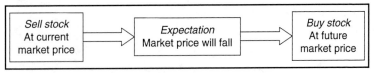

Figure 10.2: trading or investing in stocks

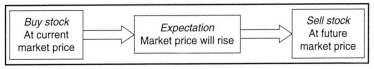

In the same way as you have the benefit of leverage when buying call options, you also gain the benefits of leverage from buying put options. You can gain a relatively large exposure to the share price movement for only a fraction of the cost. The percentage fall in the underlying stock will result in a significantly larger percentage increase in your put option value, if your put option is in-the-money. We examine this scenario in example 10.1.

Example 10.1

You are speculating that there will be a large fall in the market price of CBA in the next two months. You decided to purchase 30 $49.00 CBA put options for $1.40 when the market price of CBA was $50.00.

Two months later on option expiry, your prediction has proven correct and the price of CBA has fallen $3.75 to $46.25. Your call option is now worth $2.75.

Comparing the return on your investment to short selling the shares, we have the following results.

	Options	*Short selling*
Initial investment	30 options	3 000 shares
Opening price	$1.40	$50.00

Opening value	$4 200.00	$150 000.00
Price on expiry	$2.75	$46.25
Value on expiry	$8 250.00	$138 750.00
Net profit	$4 050.00	$11 250.00
Net change per unit	$1.35	$3.75
Percentage return*	96%	8%
* Does not account for transaction costs.		

As you can see from example 10.1, the percentage returns from put options are magnified compared to the percentage return in the movement of the market value of the stock. This example is provided to show how put options provide you with leverage. However, it is difficult to compare the two strategies as they are very different in terms of their attributes and risk profiles.

Strategy 2: limit your risk

Using put options allows you to speculate on a fall in the market price with limited risk. When buying put options, the most you can ever lose on your transaction is the total premium you paid for the options. In contrast, if you were to short sell a share, your losses would be equal to the value of any increase in the price of that share until you closed your position, regardless of how much the share price might increase.

Strategy 3: protect your existing long position

If you hold shares, there will be times when you believe these shares may fall in value. Many investors respond to this scenario in one of two ways:

⇨ Sell the shares.

⇨ Ride out the fall and hope the price recovers.

Fortunately, the savvy investor has a third option. Buying put options gives you the ability to protect the overall value of your shares without the need to sell them.

There may be a number of reasons you do not wish to sell your shares, even though you believe that there is going to be a correction in the market price of those shares. These reasons may include the following:

⇨ You may not wish to incur the transaction costs of selling and later repurchasing the shares.

⇨ You may not wish to lose your entitlement to the dividend income on those shares.

⇨ You may not wish to incur a tax liability on the sale.

⇨ Like all other traders, you cannot be 100 per cent sure that there will be a fall, or be exactly sure when it will happen.

Buying put options overcomes many of these issues. When buying put options you do not need to sell your shares, so you keep your entitlement to any dividends that may be declared. You do not incur a tax liability on sale and if the share price in fact moves up, you will still benefit from this price rise.

Buying put options to protect an existing position is a hedging strategy and a bit like buying insurance for your shares. You are locking in a selling price for your shares. Any falls in the market value of your shares will be offset against an increase in the value of your put options. No matter how far the share price falls, your share holding is protected at the strike price.

If the price of the underlying shares fall, you still have three alternative courses of action available to you.

⇨ You can keep your shares, sell your options and realise a profit to offset the fall in value of your shares.

⇨ You can exercise your options and sell your shares at the exercise price.

⇨ You can wait until closer to the expiry date to determine your course of action.

Example 10.2 illustrates how put options can reduce your losses on an existing stock holding that falls in value.

Example 10.2

You currently hold 2000 shares in NAB. You feel that the stock market is looking bearish and wish to protect your NAB holding against an expected fall in value. NAB is currently trading at $25.00 per share.

You decide to purchase 20 $25.00 NAB put options for $1.75 so that you can protect your profits so far. These options have six months to expiry.

Three months later the share price of NAB is trading at $19.50 and your put options are worth $5.90.

	Options	*Shares*
Initial investment	20 options	2 000 shares
Unit cost	$1.75	$25.00
Cost	$3 500.00	$50 000.00
Current price	$5.90	$19.50
Current value	$11 800.00	$39 000.00
Net profit/(loss)*	$8 300.00	($11 000.00)

* Net profit does not account for transaction costs.

As you can see from example 10.2, the value of your share holding fell by $11 000 at the same time that the value of your put options increased to $11 800. Including the $3500 option premium that you paid in order to protect your share value, your net loss so far is $2700 compared with a loss of $11 000 if you had not purchased the put options. You now have a choice to make.

⇨ You can sell your options. If you feel that the market has reached a base and that the share price of NAB will stabilise and start to move back up, you can sell your options. You no longer wish to have this protection and can realise the $8300 profit you made on your put options. All going well, you will also benefit if the price of NAB does in fact move back up.

⇨ You can exercise your options. If you decide that you no longer wish to hold NAB shares, you can exercise your options and sell your NAB shares for $25.00 per share, even though they are now only worth $19.50. Your $3500.00 'insurance policy' (the cost of your put options) has saved you $11 000.00 in lost value on your NAB shares.

⇨ You can wait and then either sell your options, roll over your options or exercise your options closer to the expiry date.

⇨ If you believe that NAB will continue to fall in price, you may decide to continue holding your options. You would do this if you believed that the market value of NAB will fall by more than the time value of $0.40 left in your put options before the expiry date. You will still need to decide to either sell your options, roll over your options or exercise your options before they expire. If you do not sell or exercise, your options will expire worthless, even though they contain significant intrinsic value.

Another example of using put options as insurance against a fall in value of an existing share holding in illustrated in example 10.3.

Example 10.3

You currently hold 2000 shares in NAB. You feel that the stock market is looking bearish and wish to protect your NAB holding against an expected fall in value. NAB is currently trading at $25.00 per share.

You are prepared to cover a fall in NAB of $1.00 to reduce the cost of protecting an even greater fall. So you decide to purchase 20 $24.00 NAB put options for $0.70 so that you can protect the value of your NAB shares if the price falls below $24.00. These options have three months to expiry.

Three months later the share price of NAB has only fallen slightly to $24.50 and your put options are worthless as they are still out-of-the-money.

	Options	**Shares**
Initial investment	20 options	2 000 shares
Unit cost	$0.70	$25.00
Cost	$1 400.00	$50 000.00
Current price	$0.00	$24.50
Current value	$0.00	$49 000.00
Net profit/(loss)*	($1 400.00)	($1 000.00)

* Net profit does not account for transaction costs.

In example 10.3, your put options have cost you $1400 and your shares have fallen by $1000 in value. However, your trading strategy was to insure against falls below $24. Although the price of NAB did not fall this far, you still achieved your objective. You were happy to pay $1400 to protect your share holding against a fall in value below $24.

Your hedging strategy is insuring against a potential risk. However, if this risk does not eventuate and your shares actually increase in value, you still benefit from this increase. This would not be the case if you had sold your shares instead of buying a put option.

You now need to assess if you wish to continue to hedge against a potential fall in the share price by rolling over your put option into another put option position, or you may have revised your analysis and no longer wish to enter into another hedging strategy.

In example 10.4 we use the same scenario as in the previous example, but look at the benefit of this strategy when the share price actually rises.

Example 10.4

You currently hold 2000 shares in NAB. You feel that the stock market is looking bearish and wish to protect your NAB holding against an expected fall in value. NAB is currently trading at $25.00 per share.

You are prepared to cover a fall in NAB of $1.00 to reduce the cost of protecting an even greater fall. So you decide to purchase 20 $24.00 NAB put options for $0.70 so that you can protect the value of your NAB shares if the price falls below $24.00. These options have three months to expiry.

Three months later the share price of NAB has in fact continued to rise and is now $26.00. Your put options are worthless as they are still out-of-the-money.

	Options	*Shares*
Initial investment	20 options	2 000 shares
Unit cost	$0.70	$25.00
Cost	$1 400.00	$50 000.00
Current price	$0.00	$26.00
Current value	$0.00	$52 000.00
Net profit/(loss)*	($1 400.00)	$2 000.00

* Net profit does not account for transaction costs.

In example 10.4, if you had decided to sell your NAB shares in anticipation of a fall in value, rather than buying the put options as insurance, you would not have benefited from the increase in value of your NAB shares.

In this example, your put options have cost you $1400 but your shares have actually increased in value by $2000, so even though you were hedging against a potential fall in the market value of NAB, you were still able to benefit from the resulting increase.

Once again, you now need to assess if you wish to continue to hedge against a potential fall in the share price by rolling over your put option into another put option position. Perhaps you still feel that the market will fall and you were too early, or perhaps you have revised your analysis and no longer wish to enter into another hedging strategy.

When selecting a put option to protect your current position, the choice will essentially come down to how much you are willing to pay for the options and how long you want the protection for. Options that provide a higher level of protection (a higher strike price) over a longer period (later expiry date) will have higher premiums.

Strategy 4: speculate for profit

Buying put options is a popular trading strategy for generating a profit from a falling stock price. You are speculating on the price of the underlying stock falling by a sufficient amount to cover your option premium and create an increase in the intrinsic value of the put option. In this strategy, you do not need to hold the underlying stock as you have no intention of exercising the option. Your strategy is to buy the put option and sell it for a profit before it expires.

The conditions you should look for in selecting a put option for short-term profit are the same that we looked at for selecting a call option for short-term profit.

⇨ The strike price should be close to the current market value of the stock.

⇨ The time to expiry must be sufficient.

⇨ Options with low time value in the premium will have less time decay but are also less likely to produce a profit.

Risks and disadvantages of buying put options

The risks and disadvantages in buying put options are similar to buying call options.

⇨ risk always limited to the premium you paid

⇨ limited time to expiry

⇨ time decay

⇨ fall in volatility.

Other strategies for profiting from a falling stock price include short selling and selling call options. However, the risk profile for these strategies is very different. Short selling and selling call options exposes you to unlimited risk.

Selecting your put option

In selecting your put option, it is not enough to correctly predict that the market value of the underlying stock will fall. You are speculating on a large enough movement to occur within the limited life of your option. Even if you correctly pick the downward movement within your time frame, this will be offset by the reduction in time value of your option.

Low priced options that are out-of-the-money have a lower risk and time value, and will require a much larger movement in the price of the underlying stock to create any intrinsic value. The market is efficient in re-pricing options to account for market expectations, time to expiry and the movement in price of the underlying stock. So, low priced options are cheap for a reason. There is little time value in the option as there is only a small chance that the options will create any intrinsic value before they expire.

If you buy an in-the-money put option, any movement in the underlying stock price to the downside will create a dollar for dollar profit in your put option (less time decay). However, any increase in the market value of the underlying stock will also directly reduce the value of your put option as long as it remains in-the-money.

Tip

It is erroneous to believe that cheap options are always bargains. Cheap options are out-of-the-money and more likely to expire worthless.

You need to consider the same factors in selecting your put option as you consider when selecting a call option. These factors include the following:

⇨ strike price in relation to the current market value

⇨ expiry date

⇨ volatility of the underlying stock price

⇨ option premium.

These factors were covered in chapter 9 in relation to call options.

Some general guidelines you can use in selecting your put option are as follows:

⇨ A put option with a higher strike price will:

   ¤ require a smaller fall in the share price to generate a profit

   ¤ be more expensive than a similar dated option with a lower strike price.

⇨ A put option with a longer expiry date will:

   ¤ give you a greater chance of achieving a profit on your put option as you have more time for the underlying stock price to move sufficiently in your favour

   ¤ be more expensive than a put option with a shorter expiry date as it has a higher time value.

⇨ Buying an out-of-the-money put option is consistent with a very bearish view of the underlying stock as you need a large decrease in price to generate a profit on your put option.

⇨ Buying an at-the-money or in-the-money put option is a less bearish view, but still requires a fall in value of the underlying stock price over and above the time value in the put option.

Your challenge in selecting a put option is to:

⇨ determine how far you believe the underlying stock price will fall

⇨ determine how long you think it will take to fall to that price

⇨ find put options that have a strike price and expiry date that fit with your analysis

⇨ calculate your break-even point based on premiums available

⇨ find the least expensive option that meets the criteria outlined above and will generate a sufficient return on investment.

Example 10.5 illustrates the danger of buying options that are deep out-of-the-money.

Example 10.5

You want to speculate on the price of BHP falling in the next two months. You decide to purchase a put option for $0.50 that is $3.00 out-of-the-money. BHP is trading at $45.00.

Shortly after purchasing your option, the price of BHP fell by $2.00; however, it then remained fairly flat and was priced at $42.80 on expiry.

Your option is worthless at expiry as it is still out-of-the-money.

In example 10.5, even though you correctly forecast a fall in the price of BHP, your choice of option required a fall of at least $3.50 ($0.50 premium plus the option was $3.00 out-of-the-money) before you generated any profit in your option. As the price of BHP only fell by $2.20 before expiry, your option expired worthless.

Example 10.6 shows how your option selection will affect your outcome based on the same scenario as in example 10.5.

Example 10.6

You want to speculate on the price of BHP falling in the next two months. You decide to purchase 20 put options for $3.50 that are $2.00 in-the-money. BHP is trading at $45.00.

Shortly after purchasing your option, the price of BHP fell by $2.00.

Your put options are now worth $5.45. Rather than wait to expiry as time decay is accelerating, you decide to sell your options now and realise a profit of $2.00 per option.

Put option cost	$7 000.00
Sale value	$8 900.00
Profit*	$1 900.00

* Net profit does not account for transaction costs.

In example 10.6, the higher priced option created a profit that could be realised in a very short space of time compared with the lower priced option in example 10.5 that expired worthless. Of course, circumstances will vary and your speculation on the extent and timing of movement in the price of the underlying stock will determine which options to buy.

Chapter summary

⇨ Buying a put option gives you the right, but not the obligation, to sell a stock at the strike price any time before the option expiry.

⇨ Buying put options is a strategy you can use to profit from an expected fall in market prices.

⇨ It is not necessary to actually own the underlying stock to buy a put option.

⇨ In order to profit from buying a put option, the market value of the underlying stock must fall sufficiently to offset time decay and create an increase in the intrinsic value of the option before the option expires.

⇨ There are four main reasons you might buy a put option:

  ¤ gain leverage

  ¤ limit your risk

  ¤ protect your existing long position

  ¤ speculate for profit.

⇨ As put options cost a fraction of the price of the underlying stock, they provide you with leverage. Movements in the underlying stock will result in a much larger percentage movement in the option premium, but only when the option is in-the-money.

⇨ Short selling is another strategy that can be used to profit from a falling market. However, short selling has unlimited risk and various regulatory restrictions.

⇨ Put options allow you to limit your risk, as the most you can ever lose from buying a put option is the premium you paid.

⇨ Put options can be used in a hedging strategy to offset a potential fall in value of an existing stock holding. You can protect the value of your portfolio without having to actually sell your shares.

⇨ Put options are a popular strategy for short-term speculation in a falling market. You are speculating that the price of the underlying stock will fall sufficiently to offset any time decay and increase the intrinsic value of your option.

⇨ When selecting your put options, you need to consider the following factors:

☐ strike price

☐ expiry date

☐ volatility of the underlying stock price

☐ option premium.

⇨ Low priced options are cheap as they are out-of-the-money and are more likely to expire worthless.

chapter 11

Strategies for selling covered call options

Selling call options can be high risk or quite conservative, depending on whether you own the underlying stock or not and how you structure your trade. If you sell call options and you own the underlying stock, you are selling covered call options. This is a conservative strategy with limited risk. If you sell call options and you do not own the underlying stock, you are selling uncovered or naked call options. This is a high risk strategy with potentially unlimited risk.

In this chapter we will discuss the general characteristics, advantages and disadvantages of selling covered call options. We will also discuss several different strategies that can be used and the risks attached to these strategies. As selling naked call options has a very different risk profile, this is discussed in chapter 12.

Selling covered call options is a strategy in which you can earn an income in the form of option premiums received. This is particularly effective as a strategy when stock prices remain flat or within a narrow trading range. This strategy allows you to generate additional income from your stock position without relying on capital growth.

If considering selling covered call options, it is important to assess if this strategy is appropriate for you and your investment objectives. This involves developing an understanding of how to implement a call selling strategy and the risks involved, and having an appropriate level of experience in the stock market.

Selling call options

When selling call options, you reverse the order of a usual investment or trading transaction. You open your position by selling the options first, and then one of three courses of action will occur:

⇨ You can purchase the option back later to close your position.

⇨ The option expires worthless so that you don't need to purchase it back at all.

⇨ The option is exercised against you.

Let's have a look at this process in figure 11.1.

Figure 11.1: transaction order for selling call options

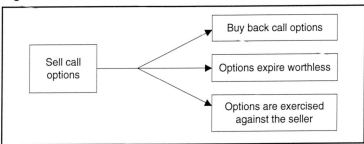

Time is a significant advantage to call option sellers. Just as time works against an option buyer, it works for the option seller. For an option seller to lose money through the sale of a call option, the market value of the underlying stock price must increase by a sufficient amount to offset both the time decay and produce an increase in the intrinsic value of the options. And this must be achieved within the limited life of the option before it expires.

Tip

Time works on your side as a call option writer (seller).

An option that contains a higher time value in the option premium has a higher potential profit for the option seller. The greater the time decay in an option, the better it is for the option seller.

As a writer (seller) of covered call options for income, you are hoping that the value of the underlying stock will remain steady and below the strike price of the option. In this scenario, the option will have no intrinsic value and will not be exercised. The value of your underlying stock will also remain steady and not lose value. If the market value of the underlying stock remains below the strike price to expiry, the option will expire worthless and you, the writer, will retain the option premium as profit.

Tip

As an option writer, your profits are essentially the declining time value that the buyer experiences over the life of the option.

When you sell a call option, you are granting the option buyer the right to buy 100 shares of the underlying stock at the strike price at any time before the option expires. This means that you are taking on this obligation and assume the risk of being required to deliver those 100 shares in the event that your option is exercised.

As an option writer, you have no control over if or when your option might be exercised. This is the buyer's right. If your call is out-of-the-money, so that the market value of the shares is below the strike price, then your call will not be exercised. However, your risk becomes evident when the market value of the underlying stock moves above the strike price of the option.

It is important to note that as a call option writer, you do not have the obligation to keep your option position open to expiry. You can close your option position at any time before expiry by buying back the same option.

There are several possible outcomes for an option writer. The actions you might take as an option writer will depend on how the value of your option changes and what your expectations are for the time remaining on the option.

If your call options remain out-of-the-money, you can either:

⇨ hold your call options to expiry, at which time they will expire worthless and you will keep the option premium as a profit

⇨ close your option position at any time by buying back the options at their current market value.

If the market value of the underlying stock moves above the strike price and your call options move into the money, you are at risk of having your options exercised at any time. At this point the following choices are available:

⇨ You can continue to hold the open option position. You may be happy to sell your stock at the strike price, or you may feel the price will fall and you decide to run the risk of the options being exercised to see the option move back out-of-the-money.

⇨ You can close your option position at any time by buying back the options at their current market value.

⇨ You can roll your position to a new option with a higher strike price and later expiry date. This involves simultaneously buying back your open position and selling a new one.

If your options are in-the-money at expiry, they will most likely be exercised and you will be obligated to deliver the underlying stock at the strike price.

Tip

When selling call options, it is very important to understand the risks and potential for loss in order to effectively manage your position.

Selling covered call options

As a stock investor, you will experience periods of time during which the price of your shares remains flat, or within a narrow trading range. During this time, you will not experience any growth on your investment and the only gains you will receive will be from any dividends paid during that time. If you believe that your shares are unlikely to move significantly, most investors would simply assess one of two options:

⇨ Hold your shares to receive any dividends to be paid and hope that the shares will eventually increase in value.

⇨ Sell the shares and invest your capital in other shares or investments that are likely to produce a better return.

However, selling covered call options gives you a third course of action that will enable you to earn income from your investment even when the value of your shares is not increasing.

When writing covered call options, your option is 'covered' by the underlying stock that you already hold. In writing covered call options, you are granting the right to the buyer to purchase your underlying stock at the strike price. To ensure that you meet this obligation in the event of your options being exercised, you are required to lodge your stock with ASX Clear. (Your broker will do this on your behalf.) If your options are exercised, ASX Clear will deliver the shares to the counterparty that exercised the option and forward the purchase price to your account.

While your shares are lodged as security for your covered calls, you are unable to sell them. You do, however, still retain ownership of the stock (unless your option is exercised) and will receive any dividend entitlements that arise during that time.

If you are considering selling covered calls, you need to consider the following:

⇨ You should have an expectation that the market price of your underlying shares will remain flat or may fall.

⇨ A decrease in the volatility of the market price of the underlying stock will be advantageous to you.

⇨ If the market price of the underlying shares increases above the strike price, you may be obligated to sell your shares at the strike price, which would be below the current market price.

⇨ Your profit potential is limited even if your shares increase significantly in value.

Following are three key strategies you can use when writing covered calls:

⇨ *Provide a source of income from the option premium.* If your view is that the market price of your stock is likely to stay flat or within a consistent trading range, selling call options over this stock can provide you with revenue from the option premium when your shares are not producing any capital gains.

⇨ *Provide some protection from a fall in value of your stock.* If you are concerned that the value of the shares might fall but do not wish to sell them at the present time, writing covered calls over those shares will provide income that can be offset against the fall in value, thus providing you with some downside protection and limiting your overall loss.

⇨ *Potentially sell your shares above the market value.* You can write a call option to sell your shares at the strike price you are happy to receive. If the market value of the underlying shares moves above this price and your options are exercised, you receive both the option premium and the strike price for your shares.

Strategy 1: provide a source of income from the option premium

To generate an income stream from selling covered calls, you must have the view that the market price of your underlying shares will remain flat, or at least below the strike price of your option. This will allow you to retain the option premium as income when the options expire worthless, and the value of your underlying shares will remain steady. This strategy is examined in example 11.1.

Example 11.1

You own 4000 WBC shares that are currently trading at $21.30. You feel the market price is going to remain fairly steady and will not move over $22.50 in the next three months.

You decide to sell 40 covered call options for $0.50 with a strike price of $22.50 and three months to expiry.

Over the next three months, the market value of WBC traded between $21.00 and $22.00 and was trading at $21.80 on expiry date.

> **Example 11.1 *(cont'd)***
>
> The options expire worthless.
>
> | | |
> |---|---:|
> | Option sale price | $0.50 |
> | Total proceeds on sale | $2 000.00 |
> | Option value on expiry | $0.00 |
> | Profit on selling covered call options* | $2 000.00 |
>
> * Profit does not include transaction costs.

As your options were never in-the-money (the market value of WBC never rose above the strike price of $22.50), there was never any chance of your options being exercised. Your options expired worthless, so as the option writer you retain the option premium of $2000.00. Your covered call strategy has earned you an extra $2000.00 more than if you had simply held your shares.

In addition, the market value of your underlying shares increased from $21.30 to $21.80, creating an unrealised gain on those shares of $0.50 per share or $2000.00.

Tip

The best possible outcome when selling covered call options is when the market value of the underlying stock is at or just below the strike price of your call option. When this occurs, you will have two positive outcomes:

⇨ *Your shares have not fallen in value.*

⇨ *You retain the full option premium.*

Strategy 2: provide some protection from a fall in value of your stock

Selling covered calls when the market value of your underlying stock is falling will provide you with premium income that you can use to offset the fall in value of your stock. You must determine that the strategy for holding your shares, even though you are expecting them to fall, is valid. This is quite often the case for a longer term investment strategy and an expected short-term retracement in price. Next, you need to determine how much protection you want to have and select your option accordingly. We consider this strategy in example 11.2.

Example 11.2

You own 4000 WBC shares that are currently trading at $21.30. You are concerned that the market is weak and your shares are going to fall in value, but you want to hold them for the longer term.

You decide to sell 40 covered call options for $0.50 with a strike price of $22.50 and three months to expiry. This will protect you against a fall of up to $0.50 in the value of WBC.

Over the next three months, the market value of WBC does in fact fall to $20.50. The options expire worthless.

Option sale price	$0.50
Total proceeds on sale	$2 000.00
Market value of WBC on sale date	$85 200.00
Market value of WBC on expiry date	$82 000.00
Total fall in value	($3 200.00)
Net loss on options and shares*	($1 200.00)

* Loss does not include transaction costs.

In example 11.2 you can see how selling the covered call options generated a return of $2000 that offset the fall in value of the underlying stock of $3200. As the call option premium was $0.50, this will cover up to a $0.50 fall in the underlying stock price. As the total fall in the underlying stock price was $0.80, the overall loss over this period was reduced to $0.30 per share or $1200 through the use of this strategy.

To gain a higher level of protection, you would need to sell a higher priced call option. This would be an option that had a longer expiry date (therefore a higher time value) or a lower strike price.

Strategy 3: potentially sell your shares above the market value

To achieve a better sale price from selling covered calls, instead of selling your shares at your target price, you sell a covered call option which has a strike price equal to your target sale price. Rather than receiving your target price on sale, you sell your shares at your target price and receive your call option premium. This is, of course, only if your options are exercised. We consider this strategy in example 11.3.

Example 11.3

You own 4000 WBC shares that are currently trading at $21.30. You believe they may go up to about $22.50 and would be happy to sell at that price.

You decide to sell 40 covered call options for $0.50 with a strike price of $22.50 and three months to expiry.

Over the next three months, the market value of WBC moves to $22.75. Your options are exercised.

You sold your WBC shares for the strike price of $22.50, plus received the option premium of $0.50, giving you total proceeds of $23.00 per share, which is higher than your target price of $22.50.

In example 11.3 you received a total of $23.00 per share, which is also $0.25 above the current market price of $22.75. In this example, your total proceeds were limited to $23.00. Regardless of how high the market price of WBC may have moved above $23.00, you would have forgone any potential profit above $23.00.

In this strategy, the most you will ever receive for your shares is the strike price plus the premium.

Tip

Whenever you calculate your profit or loss on writing covered call options, you need to account for both the option and the underlying shares.

Risks and disadvantages of selling covered call options

There are a few risks and disadvantages to selling covered call options that you need to be aware of. The most significant risk is that there may be a large fall in the price of your underlying stock. This will result in a loss in value on this stock that will only be partly offset by the option premium you received. As the stock is being held as collateral for your call options, you are unable to sell this stock until you either close your option position or the option expires. We examine this situation in example 11.4.

Example 11.4

You own 4000 WBC shares that are currently trading at $21.30. You are concerned that the market is weak and your shares are going to fall in value, but you want to hold them for the longer term.

You decide to sell 40 covered call options for $0.50 with a strike price of $22.50 and three months to expiry. This will cover a fall of $0.50 in the value of your shares.

Over the next three months, the market value of WBC decreases on some unexpected news and plummets to $19.00.

Example 11.4 *(cont'd)*

Option sale price	$0.50
Total proceeds on sale	$2 000.00
Market value of WBC on sale date	$85 200.00
Market value of WBC on option expiry	$76 000.00
Loss on WBC	($9 200.00)
Net loss on options and shares*	($7 200.00)

* Loss does not include transaction costs.

In example 11.4 you would be watching the value of your shares fall significantly, but as they are being held as security, you would be unable to sell them. You are not, however, completely helpless in this situation. You can either buy put options or buy back the options to close your position and then sell your WBC shares.

Another disadvantage of selling covered call options is that they limit the profit you can make on your underlying shares. If your analysis is incorrect, and the market price of the underlying stock has a large unexpected increase placing your options in-the-money, your options may be exercised. Upon exercise, you would be required to sell your underlying shares at the strike price of the option, missing out on the increased value above the strike price. This is referred to as an opportunity cost. It is not a realised loss that you incur, but a profit (or opportunity) that you miss out on. Example 11.5 considers this situation.

Example 11.5

You own 4000 WBC shares that are currently trading at $21.30. You are concerned that the market is weak and your shares are going to fall in value but you want to hold them for the longer term.

You decide to sell 40 covered call options for $0.50 with a strike price of $22.50 and three months to expiry.

Over the next three months, the market value of WBC actually increases on some unexpected news and rises to $24.25. Your options are exercised.

Option sale price	$0.50
Total proceeds on sale	$2 000.00
Market value of WBC on option sale date	$85 200.00
Strike price value of WBC on exercise	$90 000.00
Profit on sale of WBC*	$4 800.00
Total profit options and shares*	$6 000.00
Current market value of WBC	$97 000.00
Forgone capital gain	$7 000.00
Net forgone gain	$5 000.00

* Profit does not include transaction costs.

In example 11.5 you still profit on the sale of your underlying stock and retain the option premium, netting a total profit before transaction costs of $6000. However, if you had not sold the covered call and kept your WBC shares, they would now be worth $97 000. You would have had an unrealised gain of $7000, without the $2000 option premium. So your net forgone profits are $5000.

Tip

You are taking a definite premium income now to forgo a potential gain during the life of the option.

You are not obligated to hold your covered call options to expiry. If the market price of the underlying stock increases towards the strike price, or moves above the strike price, you may consider buying back your options at a loss. This would eliminate the risk that your options will be exercised if you did not wish this to happen.

Although it is more likely that your options will be exercised close to the expiry date, this is not always the case. If your option is in-the-money, you need to accept that it may be exercised at any time. You also need to be aware of any ex-dividend dates, as your options will be more likely to be exercised if the underlying stock is about to go ex-dividend.

Tip

When your option moves into the money, you need to either accept the risk of exercise, or buy back options to close your position.

Selecting your covered call option

Once you have decided upon your covered call option strategy and understand the risks involved, you need to decide on which call option to write. For any stock, you will have a range of exercise prices and expiry dates to choose from.

The lower the strike price, the larger the premium you will receive. This will provide you with a higher income and more protection against a downside move in the underlying stock. However, the lower strike price also means that you will receive a lower price for your shares if the market value increases and your options are exercised.

Your choice of strike price will be dependent upon your view of the market value of your underlying shares and your reasons for writing the covered calls. If you have a very bearish view and are concerned about protecting your downside risk, a lower strike price fits with this view. If your view is more neutral and you wish to hold your stock, you will need to select a strike price that you believe will keep your options out-of-the-money for the life of the option.

Longer dated options will have higher premiums but they also increase the time over which the options may move into the money and be exercised. Your risk here is that the underlying stock has a longer time in which to break out of its current trading range before the expiry date of your option. If the stock price moves unexpectedly either up or down, this will work against your covered call strategy.

Whenever you write a covered call option, you need to be prepared to have the option exercised. There is always the risk of your option being exercised if the call is in-the-money. Up until now, all of our examples have involved selling covered calls that are out-of-the-money. However, this does not preclude you from selling calls in-the-money for short-term profit. You do, however, need to be comfortable with the risk that your options may be exercised at any time that they remain in-the-money. This scenario is examined in example 11.6.

Example 11.6

You own 2000 shares that recently rose in price from $29.00 to $31.00. You feel that the share price is due for a short-term retracement in price.

You decide to sell 20 covered call options with a strike price of $28.00 for a premium of $4.50 and three months to expiry.

The price of the shares fell by $2.00 in the next month back to $29.00.

You decide to close out your options, which are now worth $2.20.

Option sale price	$9 000.00
Buy back price	$4 400.00
Total profit on options*	$4 600.00
Fall in value of the shares	($4 000.00)
Total profit on options and shares*	$600.00

* Profit does not include transaction costs.

In example 11.6 you received $4.50 in premium for the obligation to sell your shares at $3.00 below the current market value. As your option is in-the-money, any fall in the underlying stock price will result in a dollar for dollar fall in intrinsic value of your options.

Your decision to sell your options has netted you a tidy short-term profit in addition to offsetting the fall in value of your underlying stock. It is important to note that the options may have been exercised before you were able to sell them, as is revealed in example 11.7.

Example 11.7

You own 2000 shares that recently rose in price from $29.00 to $31.00. You feel that the share price is due for a short-term retracement in price.

You decide to sell 20 covered call options with a strike price of $28.00 for a premium of $4.50 and three months to expiry.

The price of the shares fell by $2.00 in the next month back to $29.00.

You decide to close out your options, which are now worth $2.20; however, your options are exercised before you can sell.

Option sale price	$9 000.00
Market value of shares when options sold	$62 000.00
Strike price of shares	$56 000.00
Net loss on your shares	($6 000.00)
Total profit on options and shares*	$3 000.00

* Profit does not include transaction costs.

Following are some conditions for you to be aware of when selecting your covered call option:

⇨ *The strike price of the option is higher than the original cost of your underlying shares.* This will ensure you make a profit on both your option and your shares if the option is exercised.

⇨ *The call is in-the-money, but not deep in-the-money.* This will mean that the option has intrinsic value that will move one to one with movements in the underlying stock price. This provides an opportunity to close your option position for a short-term profit.

⇨ *The call is out-of-the-money but not deep out-of-the-money.* This will mean that the total option premium is time value and the time value will be higher than if the option was deep out-of-the-money. As long as the underlying stock price remains below the strike price until expiry, you will retain the full option premium as profit.

⇨ *The time to expiry.* The time to expiry needs to be long enough to create time value in your option when you sell it, but not too long to reduce the risk of the options moving into the money.

⇨ *The option premium.* The premium you receive for your option needs to be large enough to compensate you for taking on the risks of an option writer.

When selecting your covered call option, you need to consider all of the following factors:

⇨ your strategy for selling the call option

⇨ the premium you will receive

⇨ the mix of time value and intrinsic value in the premium

⇨ time left to expiry

⇨ your expectation of movement in the price of the underlying stock in the time left to expiry

⇨ the gap between the current market price of the underlying stock and the strike price of the option.

In managing your covered call position you also need to consider your objectives in holding the underlying stock as well as your call option strategy. This will influence your decision to close out an option position or to continue to hold it when it is approaching or is already in-the-money.

Chapter summary

⇨ Covered call options exist when you write an option over underlying shares that you already own.

⇨ When selling call options, you sell your option first for a premium. The option position can then be closed, may be exercised by the buyer or may expire worthless.

⇨ Time is an advantage to option sellers. The higher the time value in an option, the greater the potential profit for the option seller.

⇨ As a writer of covered call options, you are hoping that the value of the underlying stock will remain steady.

⇨ When writing call options, you have no control over if and when the option might be exercised.

⇨ You are not obligated to keep your option position open to expiry. You can close out at any time by purchasing the call option.

⇨ When writing covered call options, the underlying stock will be held by ASX Clear and you will be unable to sell it while the option position remains open.

⇨ A decrease in the volatility of the market price of the underlying stock will be advantageous.

⇨ If the market price of the underlying shares increases above the strike price, you may be obligated to sell your shares at the strike price, which will be below the current market price.

⇨ The key strategies you can use when writing covered calls are:

⨉ provide a source of income from the option premium

⨉ provide some protection from a fall in the value of your stock

⨉ potentially sell your shares above the market value.

⇨ The best outcome when selling covered calls for income is that the market value of the underlying stock remains flat and below the strike price of the option.

⇨ The most significant risk when selling covered call options is a fall in the value of your underlying stock. The loss on your stock value will only be partly offset by your option premium.

⇨ Selling covered call options will also limit your potential profit. A large rise in the share price of the underlying stock above the strike price will result in you selling your shares below their current market value. You will not benefit from the increase in the underlying stock price.

⇨ Your choice of call option will be dependent upon your view of the market value of your underlying shares and your reasons for writing the covered calls.

⇨ Whenever you write a covered call option, you need to be prepared to have the option exercised.

⇨ When selecting your covered call option, you need to consider all of the following factors:

⨉ your strategy for selling the call option

⨉ the premium you will receive

⨉ the mix of time value and intrinsic value in the premium

⌗ the time left to expiry

⌗ your expectation of movement in the price of the underlying stock in the time left to expiry

⌗ the gap between the current market price of the underlying stock and the strike price of the option.

chapter 17

Strategies for selling naked call options

Selling naked call options, or uncovered calls, is a strategy whereby you sell call options but do not own the underlying stock. This is a high risk strategy as your losses are potentially unlimited. Because of the high risk profile of selling naked call options, this strategy is only recommended for traders who have enough experience and skill in the market to manage such a position.

In this chapter we will discuss the advantages and disadvantages of selling naked call options and some of the strategies that can be used.

Selling naked call options

When selling a naked call option, you are granting the right to the buyer to purchase 100 shares of the underlying stock at the strike price. So what happens if your option moves into the money and is exercised?

Theoretically, you are required to deliver the stock to the option holder. You would need to buy the stock at the prevailing market price, and then sell it to the option holder at the strike price. This would result in a loss to the option seller, as the option will only be exercised if the market price of the underlying stock is higher than the strike price of the option. And this is where the unlimited risk comes in. As there is no theoretical limit on how high the price of the underlying stock can rise, there is no limit on the losses you might incur.

Tip

The settlement time for exercising an option is T+3 (three days after exercise). This is to allow time for purchase of the underlying stock (all stock settlements are T+3) if required. This is in contrast to the settlement period for buying and selling options, which is only T+1.

In practice, however, it is the settlement house, ASX Clear, that delivers the underlying stock on exercise of an option. You will recall from chapter 11 that when you sell covered call options, ASX Clear holds your stock to 'cover' your option position. If the option is exercised, ASX Clear collects the sale proceeds from the option holder and delivers the shares to them. ASX Clear then passes on the sale proceeds to the option writer.

For naked call options, upon exercise ASX Clear will buy the stock at the current market price to deliver to the option holder who exercised the option. ASX Clear would also collect the proceeds on sale of the stock at the strike price. As an option seller, your account would be debited with the difference between the cost to purchase at market value and the sale proceeds at the strike price.

When selling naked calls, you are required to provide a margin that is held by ASX Clear. This margin is calculated as the amount of security that ASX Clear deems necessary to ensure that you can meet your obligations under the option contract. This margin amount will vary with the market price and volatility of price movements of the underlying stock. ASX Clear will take the funds they require on exercise of an option from your margin first. Refer to chapter 5 for more detail on margins.

Example 12.1 shows how a loss on uncovered call options is calculated upon exercise of the options.

Example 12.1

You sell 40 WBC naked call options for $0.50 with a strike price of $22.50 and three months to expiry.

Over the next three months, the market value of WBC increases to $25.00 and your option is exercised.

Total proceeds on sale of options	$2 000.00
Current market value of 4000 WBC	$100 000.00
4000 WBC at strike price of $22.50	$90 000.00
Loss on exercise*	($10 000.00)
Net loss on options*	($8 000.00)

* Loss does not include transaction costs.

As you can see in example 12.1, your option premium of $2000 was well exceeded by the loss on exercise of the options of $10 000, giving you a net loss of $8000. If the market value of WBC had increased to $30.00, your net losses would have been $18 000.

Tip

The losses from selling naked call options can be significant if there is a significant increase in the market value of the underlying stock above the strike price.

As discussed in chapter 11, key characteristics of selling either covered call options or naked call options are:

⇨ *time.* Time is a significant advantage when selling call options due to time decay.

⇨ *control.* As the seller of an option, you have no control over when or if your option will be exercised. This is the right of the option buyer. You do, however, have the choice of closing your option position at any time before it is exercised and before expiry.

⇨ *option value.* The most significant factors that will affect the value of your option are:

  ⌑ changes in the market price of the underlying stock

  ⌑ changes in the volatility of the market price of the underlying stock

  ⌑ time remaining to expiry.

The most significant difference between selling covered call options and selling naked call options is risk. When selling covered call options and the market moves against your option position, you only incur the opportunity cost of selling below market value. However, when selling naked call options and the market moves against you, your potential losses can be significant and unlimited.

Due to the risks involved, brokers will have specific requirements that you must meet in order to sell naked call options. These will include the level of equity in your account and your experience in trading both equities and options. Generally, you will be assigned an options trading level based on your experience, which will determine what types of strategies you can use. Selling naked call options (and selling put options) will require a higher option trading level than buying options or selling covered call options.

The break-even point when selling call options is when the market value of the underlying stock is equal to the strike price of the option plus the option premium. Therefore, it is still possible for an option writer to make a profit on the sale of naked call options when they are exercised, as long as the market value of the underlying stock is less than the break-even price.

We show an example of a net profit on selling naked call options when they have been exercised in example 12.2.

Example 12.2

You sell 10 WBC naked call options for $2.50 with a strike price of $22.50 and three months to expiry. Your options are at-the-money.

Over the next three months, the market value of WBC increases to $24.00 and your option is exercised.

Total proceeds on sale of options	$2 500.00
Current market value of 1000 WBC	$24 000.00
1000 WBC at strike price of $22.50	$22 500.00
Loss on exercise*	($1 500.00)
Net profit on options*	$1 000.00

* Profit and loss do not include transaction costs.

Tip

Exercise of your option does not necessarily mean you lose on your option trade. You only realise a loss if the market value of the underlying stock is above your break-even point.

Naked call option strategies

Your aim when selling naked call options is to make a profit from your trade. In order to profit from selling naked call options, you need one of the following events to occur:

⇨ The underlying stock price remains below the strike price so that the option loses time value and expires worthless.

⇨ The underlying stock price falls so that the value of the option decreases and you can close your position at a profit.

⇨ The underlying stock price increases but by a small enough amount so that the time decay on your option offsets any other increase in time or intrinsic value.

When managing your naked call option position, you can either:

⇨ close your option position at any time before it is exercised and before it expires

⇨ hold your option position.

To close your option position you simply buy back the option at its current market price. The way in which you manage your open naked call option position will depend upon the movement in price of the underlying stock and the subsequent effect on the market value of your option.

There are four ways in which the market value of the underlying stock can move:

⇨ The value of the underlying stock falls.

⇨ The value of the underlying stock remains steady.

⇨ The value of the underlying stock increases but remains below the strike price of the option.

⇨ The value of the underlying stock increases above the strike price of the option.

The value of the underlying stock falls

When the market value of the underlying stock falls, this is good news to the seller of a naked call option. The value of the option will decrease due to time decay and the possibility that the option will move into the money is reduced.

You may wish to close your option position at this time if you wish to realise a profit on your trade by buying back the option at a lower price. You would do this only if you felt that the market value of the underlying stock will reverse and might move above the strike price of the option. As the option is now deep out-of-the-money, it is more likely that you would simply hold the option to expiry and see it expire worthless.

The value of the underlying stock remains steady

When the market value of the underlying stock remains steady, the value of the option will decrease due to time decay.

You may wish to close your option position at this time if you wish to realise a profit on your trade by buying back the option at a lower price. Once again, you would do this if you felt that the market value of the underlying stock might rebound and move above the strike price of the option.

The value of the underlying stock increases but remains below the strike price of the option

When the market value of the underlying stock increases towards the strike price of the option, the value of the option will change in two aspects:

⇨ It will increase due to a greater likelihood of the option moving into the money.

⇨ It will decrease due to time decay.

The actual change in value of the option will depend upon the interaction of these factors and may produce an increase, decrease or no change in the value of the option.

You may wish to close your option position at this time if you wish to avoid exercise and are concerned about the increased risk of the market value of the underlying stock continuing to rise.

The value of the underlying stock increases above the strike price of the option

When the market value of the underlying stock increases above the strike price of the option, the option will be *in-the-money* and exercise is likely. The value of the option will most likely increase due to an increase in intrinsic value.

You may wish to close your option position at this time to avoid exercise or further losses due to the possibility of higher increases in the value of the underlying stock price.

Tip

As an option seller, you open your option position with a sale and close your option position with a purchase.

We will now consider a couple of strategies that you can use when selling naked call options. Keep in mind that when managing any of these option strategies, you have the option to close your position at any time (as we have just detailed) based on the movement in market value of the underlying stock.

Strategy 1: selling out-of-the-money naked call options

When selling out-of-the-money naked call options, you are speculating that the value of the underlying stock will remain at or below the strike price of your option. If this occurs, your call option will expire worthless and you will retain the option premium. This strategy is outlined in example 12.3.

Example 12.3

WBC shares are currently trading at $21.30. You feel the market price is going to remain fairly steady and will not move over $22.50 in the next three months.

You decide to sell 40 covered call options for $0.50 with a strike price of $22.50 and three months to expiry.

Over the next three months, the market value of WBC traded between $21.00 and $22.00 and was trading at $21.80 on expiry date.

The options expire worthless.

Option sale price	$0.50
Total proceeds on sale	$2 000.00
Option value on expiry	$0.00
Profit on selling covered call options*	$2 000.00

* Profit does not include transaction costs.

If, however, the market value of the underlying stock increases, or you feel that the probability of an increase has become significant, you can close your option position before expiry to realise a profit on your trade and avoid potential loss or exercise. This is explained in example 12.4.

Example 12.4

You sell 10 WBC naked call options for $2.50 with a strike price of $22.50 and three months to expiry.

Over the next three months the market value of WBC has remained steady between $21.50 and $22.00; however, your analysis leads you to believe the stock is likely to break out of this trading range in the near future.

Your options are now worth only $0.30 as they are near expiry and still out-of-the-money. You decide to close your option position.

Total proceeds on sale of options	$2 500.00
Current value of options	$0.30
Cost to close option position	$300.00
Net profit on options*	$2 200.00

* Profit does not include transaction costs.

In example 12.4 you have perceived that the risk of a potential loss on your options is worth paying the $0.30 per option to close your position before expiry and you realise a profit of $2200 on the trade.

Strategy 2: selling in-the-money naked call options

Selling in-the-money naked call options is a highly speculative and risky trading strategy. As the options are in-the-money, they can be exercised at any time. You also face a one-to-one correlation between any increase in the market value of the stock and an increase in the intrinsic value of your options.

This is a strategy that should only be used by experienced traders. It can be used when you believe there will be a sudden fall in the market value of the underlying share. Any fall will result in an equivalent fall in the value of the options, which can then be closed at a profit, or potentially expire worthless if the market value of the underlying stock falls below and remains below the strike price. We explain this in example 12.5.

Example 12.5

You have noticed that the price of CSL jumped from $34.00 to $37.00 in the last few weeks. You believe that the price will hit resistance at $37.00 and fall back below $36.00 in the very near term.

You decide to sell 10 CSL naked call options for $3.50 with a strike price of $36.00 and three months to expiry.

In the next two weeks, the price of CSL does fall and is trading at $36.00. You decide to close your option position for a profit.

Total proceeds on sale of options	$4 500.00
Current value of options	$2.30
Cost to close option position	$2 500.00
Net profit on options*	$2 000.00

* Profit does not include transaction costs.

In example 12.5 the value of the options fell by $1.20, representing a loss of $1.00 of intrinsic value and $0.20 in time value. You profited one-to-one on the fall in the market value of CSL while it was in-the-money (above $36.00) plus time decay. It is important to note that your option may have been exercised at any time that the options were in-the-money.

Risks and disadvantages of selling naked call options

The most significant risk in selling naked call options is the potential for unlimited losses if the market value of the underlying stock increases above the strike price during the life of your option. However, there are two other disadvantages to be aware of.

The requirement to provide a margin against your open position is a major disadvantage associated with selling naked call options. This margin will increase if the market moves against your call option and you will be required to provide additional margin in the form of cash or securities. Generally, you will be required to provide this within 24 hours.

Another important disadvantage is that if you do suffer a loss on your option position and are unable to contribute additional funds to your account to cover the required margin, your broker may sell your existing securities to cover this loss. The sale of these securities may be poorly timed and not in line with your investment strategy.

Due to the significant risk of potentially unlimited loss from writing naked call options, it is important to assess if this strategy is appropriate for you. As we have said, writing naked call options is an extremely risky strategy and you should consider the following factors in determining if it is an appropriate strategy for you.

⇨ *Your risk profile.* You need to assess if the level of risk involved in selling naked call options is appropriate for you. This needs to be assessed in light of your ability to manage a position with the potential for significant losses, plus your financial ability to incur a worst case scenario. You do not want to wipe out your trading account from just one naked call option that moved unexpectedly.

⇨ *Your knowledge of the risk and of options.* It is important that you fully understand the risks involved and the parameters of the options you are considering writing. It is easy to become excited about the potential for profit and downplay the potential risks.

⇨ *Your trading experience.* Knowledge of a particular trading strategy is important, but it does not replace trading experience. Entering into such a high risk strategy such as selling naked calls requires you to have a reasonable level of experience in the market. Your experience in the market will guide you in selecting appropriate call options, managing the inherent risk and determining what level of risk you can handle, both emotionally and financially.

⇨ *Your capital.* When writing naked call options, you are required to provide a margin to cover your position. Thus the size of your trading account will determine the number and size of naked calls you are able to write. You also need to allow additional capital in the event of a margin call or adverse movement in market value of the underlying shares.

⇨ *Your trading and investment goals.* In crafting your overall trading and investment goals, you will have broad objectives about the types of trades you wish to enter, the level of risk you wish to take and the returns you want to generate. If you are looking for high-risk high returns, then writing naked call options may be appropriate for a portion of your total portfolio. However, if you are looking for long-term stable growth, then other strategies may be more suitable.

Chapter summary

⇨ Selling naked call options involves writing call options when you do not own the underlying shares.

⇨ This is a high risk strategy as it exposes you to significant and potentially unlimited losses.

⇨ If you write a naked call option and it is exercised by the buyer, you are required to pay the difference between the market value of the underlying shares and the strike price of the option. As there is no limit on how high a share price may rise, your losses can be significant.

⇨ When selling naked call options, you are required to provide a margin to ensure you are able to meet your obligations.

⇨ When selling naked call options, time works in your favour due to the time decay incurred by the buyer over the life of the option.

⇨ You have no control over when or if your option might be exercised. If your option is in-the-money, it might be exercised at any time.

⇨ If you no longer wish to hold your open option position, you can close your position at any time before exercise or expiry by buying the option.

⇨ Selling naked call options has a very different risk profile to selling covered call options. Selling covered calls is a conservative strategy compared with selling naked call options, which is a high risk strategy.

⇨ The break-even point is when the market value of the underlying stock is equal to the strike price of the option plus the option premium.

⇨ To profit from selling naked call options, you need one of the following events to occur:

¤ The underlying stock price remains below the strike price so that the option loses time value and expires worthless.

¤ The underlying stock price falls so that the value of the option decreases and you can close your position at a profit.

¤ The underlying stock price increases but by a small enough amount so that the time decay on your option offsets any other increase in time or intrinsic value.

⇨ When selling out-of-the-money naked call options, you are speculating that the market value of the underlying stock will remain below the strike price of your option.

⇨ Selling in-the-money naked call options is extremely high risk as the value of the option has intrinsic value and will change in line with changes in the value of the underlying stock, good or bad. This strategy should only be used by very experienced traders.

⇨ The most significant risk in selling naked call options is if your options move into the money and you are exposed to potentially unlimited losses.

⇨ You must provide a margin for your position and this margin will change in line with changes in the value of your call options.

⇨ When assessing if writing naked call options is an appropriate strategy for you, you should consider your:

¤ risk profile

¤ level of knowledge about trading and options in particular

¤ level of trading experience

¤ capital

¤ trading and investment goals.

chapter 13

Strategies for selling put options

Selling put options is a strategy you can use to profit when you expect the value of an underlying share to remain flat or increase slightly. Selling put options has the same relationship to the value of the underlying share as buying call options. The value of the underlying share increases, and so the profit on your option position increases. However, the risk profile is very different.

In this chapter we will look at the advantages and disadvantages of selling put options and also explore some of the strategies you can use when selling put options.

Selling put options

When selling a put option, you are granting the buyer the right to sell to you 100 shares of the underlying stock at the strike price. You receive a premium for accepting the risk that the option may be exercised and you will be required to purchase the underlying stock at the strike price.

Tip

As with selling a call option, when selling put options your profit is limited to the premium you receive.

The option will only be exercised by the buyer if the market value of the underlying stock is below the strike price of the option. If your options are exercised, you are required to buy the underlying stock at the strike price, which will be higher than the current market value of the stock. As a put option seller, you have no control over if or when your options may be exercised. You can, however, close your option position at any time before the option is exercised or expires.

The possible outcomes that you may face as a writer of put options are:

⇨ your option remains out-of-the-money and expires worthless

⇨ you decide to close your option position before expiry

⇨ your option moves into the money and is exercised before expiry. This will require you to purchase the underlying stock at the strike price.

Generally, the best outcome for a put option seller is if the market value of the underlying stock remains above the strike price of the option. This will result in the option expiring worthless and, as the option seller, you keep the option premium as profit. Let's consider this in example 13.1.

Example 13.1

You feel that the price of CBA is going to hold above $50 over the next two months so you decide to sell 10 $50 CBA put options for $1 when the market price of CBA is $51.

By the expiry date, the price of CBA did in fact stay above $50.

As the market value of CBA never fell below $50, your put option was never in-the-money so never at risk of being exercised.

At expiry, the put option is still out-of-the-money and expires worthless. You retain the $1000 premium as a profit on your option trade.*

* This calculation does not include transaction costs.

In example 13.1 the price of the underlying stock moved in line with your expectations and the option expired worthless. In example 13.2 let's consider the scenario if the price of the underlying stock fell, contrary to your expectations.

Example 13.2

You feel that the price of CBA is going to hold above $50.00 over the next two months so you decide to sell 10 $50.00 CBA put options for $1.00 when the market price of CBA is $51.00.

In the next month, the price of CBA falls to $48.50.

Your options are now in-the-money and are priced at $2.00. What should you do?

In example 13.2 the market value of CBA has not moved in line with your expectations and your options are now in-the-money. You have two alternatives.

⇨ You can close your option position to mitigate the risk of the options being exercised or incurring further losses if the market value of CBA continues to fall. To close your option position, you would need to purchase the put options for $2, realising a loss of $1000 on your trade (before transaction costs).

⇨ Your other alternative is to hold your option position. You would do this for one of two reasons. You might feel that the price of CBA will rebound above $50 very quickly and you are prepared to risk exercise in the short term to potentially recoup the loss on your option position. The other reason is that you may feel that $50 is a fair price for CBA and you are happy to buy the stock at this price. Your premium will offset the above market price you are paying so that the net cost of purchasing the shares is effectively $49.

Risks and disadvantages of selling put options

Selling put options carries the risk of significant losses. However, these losses do have a limit, unlike selling naked call options. The value of a put option increases as the value of the underlying stock decreases. Therefore, the maximum loss you can incur is limited to the strike price of the option. If the market value of the underlying stock fell to zero, then your loss on the option would be the value of the underlying shares at the strike price, less the premium you received on selling the put option. Although it is unlikely to happen, this is your maximum risk exposure when selling put options.

You can mitigate the risk of loss through careful selection of stocks. It is unlikely that a stock will trade below the company's net tangible assets over the longer term (although it may fall below this in the short term). Referring to the net tangible assets of the underlying stock gives you a reasonable basis in which to assess your risk when selling put options.

Another aspect to consider is the margin requirements. When you sell put options, you are required to provide a margin to ensure that you can meet your obligations under the put option. This margin will increase significantly if your put option moves into the money and is at risk of exercise. You therefore need to have ready funds available to meet any margin calls.

The third risk you face is exercise. If your put option is exercised, you need to have the full capital required to purchase the underlying stock at the strike price and commit this capital to buying those shares. This can potentially tie up your capital in stocks which you now need to manage.

Evaluating the risks of selling put options is slightly different from your risk when selling naked call options. With naked call options, you will realise a cash loss if your options are exercised. When selling put options, you need to be prepared to buy the underlying stock if your options are exercised. Although you can resell these shares on the market immediately, or whenever you choose, you must still be prepared and able to purchase them in full in the event of exercise of your options.

Selling put options strategies

There are a number of strategies you can apply when selling put options. The strategies all rely on the expectation that the value of the underlying stock will remain steady or increase in value. We will discuss the following strategies:

⇨ provide a source of income from the option premium

⇨ utilise your spare capital

⇨ purchase shares at a discount to your target price.

Strategy 1: provide a source of income from the option premium

Speculating on the price of the underlying stock to generate a short-term profit is the most popular reason for selling put options. To generate an income stream from selling put options, you must have the view that the market price of the underlying shares will remain flat and above the strike price you choose for your option. If the market value of the underlying shares does remain above the strike price of your options, they will expire worthless and you will retain the option premium as income. Consider this strategy in example 13.3.

Example 13.3

WBC shares are currently trading at $21.80 and you are speculating that the market price is going to remain fairly steady and will not move below $21.00 in the next three months.

You decide to sell 40 put options for $0.50 with a strike price of $20.50 and three months to expiry.

Over the next three months, the market value of WBC trades between $21.00 and $22.00 and was trading at $21.50 on expiry date.

The options expire worthless.

Option sale price	$0.50
Total proceeds on sale	$2 000.00
Profit on selling put options*	$2 000.00

* Profit does not include transaction costs.

As your options were never in-the-money (the market value of WBC never fell below the strike price of $20.50) in example 13.3 there was never any chance of your options being exercised. Your options expired worthless, so as the option writer you retain the option premium of $2000.00.

The situation would be different if the market value of the underlying stock fell, as you can see in example 13.4.

Example 13.4

WBC shares are currently trading at $21.80 and you are speculating that the market price is going to remain fairly steady and will not move below $21.00 in the next three months.

You decide to sell 40 put options for $0.50 with a strike price of $20.50 and three months to expiry.

> Over the next month, the market value of WBC fell to $20.00 and the put options are now worth $0.90. You decide to close your option position.
>
> | | |
> |---|---:|
> | Option sale price | $0.50 |
> | Total proceeds on sale | $2 000.00 |
> | Cost to close put option position | ($3 600.00) |
> | Loss on selling put options* | ($1 600.00) |
>
> * Loss does not include transaction costs.

In example 13.4 you closed your put options at a loss. If, however, the put options were exercised before you could close your position, you would have been obligated to purchase the underlying stock at $20.50, costing you a total of $82 000.

It is important whenever selling put options that you are prepared to buy the underlying stock at the strike price. Therefore, when choosing your put options, it is wise to select stocks that you are comfortable owning at strike prices you feel represent fair value for those stocks. You can then manage your stock position accordingly.

This does not mean that you want the options to be exercised, and may well choose to close any open put option positions that are at risk of being exercised. It does mean that you recognise that exercise of your options is a risk of selling and you are prepared to accept this risk and have a strategy if the risk eventuates. Consider the scenario in example 13.5.

Example 13.5

You have had some recent success selling put options without any being exercised. You are feeling confident and have just sold put options on five different securities to generate a significant option premium.

Example 13.5 *(cont'd)*

In the space of a few days, a global event has caused a dramatic drop across the entire stock market and all your put options fell into the money and were exercised.

You now have to provide the capital to purchase all five stocks at prices above their current market value. You have to sell some of your existing stocks at a depressed value in order to meet your obligations under the put options.

Obviously example 13.5 is a worst case scenario. However, it is important to consider this outcome as a potential risk. In this example you would have sold shares that you wanted to keep at a poor price, in order to purchase stocks below their current market values. Your portfolio would be carrying a significant unrealised loss and you would have no free capital.

Strategy 2: utilise your spare capital

This strategy is based on your speculation that the market is overvalued and you do not wish to invest at current prices. Selling put options will enable you to generate premium income, using your spare capital to meet the margins on your put options.

You will profit from the option premium if the stock price continues to rise or remains above the strike price. If the value of the underlying stock falls towards the strike price, you can either close your position, or let the option move into the money and purchase the stock at the strike price. Either way, you keep the option premium as a return on the capital you provided as margin to sell your put options.

This strategy works in the same manner as strategy 1. The difference is that this may be applied as a short-term strategy for investors with spare capital who believe the market is overvalued, rather than an ongoing strategy of speculation for profit.

Strategy 3: purchase shares at a discount to your target price

The third strategy in selling put options is to set your strike price at a target purchase price with the intention of purchasing the underlying stock at this price. This is a strategy you can use if you wish to purchase the underlying stock at a set price that is below the current market value. The advantage of selling put options is that in addition to buying the stock at your target price, you also receive the option premium. Let's consider this in example 13.6.

Example 13.6

You would like to buy 500 WBC shares at $20.00. They are currently trading at $21.80.

You decide to sell five put options for $1.80 with a strike price of $20.00 and six months to expiry.

Over the next few months, the market value of WBC falls to $19.50 and you receive notice that your options have been exercised.

Option sale price	$1.80
Total proceeds on sale	$900.00
Cost to purchase WBC at $20.00	$10 000.00
Net effective cost to buy WBC*	$9 200.00
Current market value of WBC at $19.50	$9 750.00

* Does not include transaction costs.

In example 13.6 you wanted to buy WBC when the price hit $20.00. So rather than putting in a limit order to buy the shares directly, you sold a put option. This achieved your desired outcome to buy the stock at your target price, and earned you an extra $900.00 in option premium. When using this strategy, there is the risk that your options may not be exercised. This risk is illustrated in example 13.7.

Example 13.7

You would like to buy 500 WBC shares at $20.00. They are currently trading at $21.80.

You decide to sell five put options for $1.80 with a strike price of $20.00 and six months to expiry.

Over the next few months, the market value of WBC fell to $20.10 and then rose to $22.00.

Example 13.7 illustrates the disadvantage of this strategy. If the stock price does not fall low enough for your options to be exercised, you may miss out on purchasing the stock. In selling your put options you are required to provide capital as margin, so even if you decided to buy the stock at above $20.00, you may not have the free capital to do so. In that event, you would need to close your option position first.

As a put option seller, you risk losing future profits in the following two ways.

⇨ If the price of the underlying stock rises, you lose the profits you might have gained if you had simply bought the stock directly.

⇨ If the price of the underlying stock falls dramatically, you are still required to buy the stock at the strike price if the option is exercised. You will be paying above market price and the sharp fall may change your position on this stock.

In both of these cases, you still retain the option premium as profit.

Chapter summary

⇨ Selling put options is a strategy to generate a profit if your expectation is for the value of an underlying share to remain steady or to rise slightly.

⇨ When selling put options you are granting the buyer the right to purchase the underlying stock at the strike price any time before expiry.

⇨ If you are selling put options, you must be prepared to purchase the underlying stock at the strike price. This will guide you in your selection of options.

⇨ Generally, the best outcome for a put option seller is that the price of the underlying stock remains above the strike price of your option so that your options expire worthless and you retain the option premium.

⇨ Selling put options carries the risk of significant losses. Your losses are only limited to the value of the underlying shares at the strike price. This will occur if the value of the underlying stock falls to zero.

⇨ You are required to provide a margin when selling put options to ensure you can meet your obligations in the event of exercise.

⇨ You are at risk of exercise at any time the option is in-the-money.

⇨ You should only sell put options over stocks that you would be comfortable buying at the strike price.

⇨ The three main strategies for selling put options are:

 ⌑ provide a source of income from the option premium

 ⌑ utilise your spare capital

 ⌑ purchase shares at a discount to your target price.

⇨ The most popular strategy for selling put options is to generate an income from the option premium. This involves speculating on the market value of the underlying stock remaining above the strike price of the option.

⇨ You can always close your option position before exercise and before expiry if you wish to avoid the risk of your option being exercised.

⇨ You can use spare capital as margin when selling put options as a short-term measure to earn additional income.

⇨ You can sell put options as a way to purchase stocks at your target price. You select the options based on the stock you wish to buy and the strike price at your target buy price. If your options are exercised, you achieve your objective in buying the stock and retain the option premium.

⇨ There are two risks in using put options to purchase stocks at your target price. The stock price may rise and you miss out on entering, or the stock price may fall dramatically and you are required to buy the stock well above market price.

chapter 14

Advanced strategies: using multiple option spreads

So far we have discussed single option strategies so that you can fully understand when they are appropriate and what the outcomes will be for any scenario. Once you have this understanding, there are many additional ways in which you can combine option and stock positions in an array of different strategies. Your only limitations are your available capital to meet margin requirements and your risk profile.

In this chapter, we will introduce the concept of multiple option strategies. Although multiple option strategies are based on combining two or more of the basic option strategies, they are a little more complex to understand and apply.

The three main multiple option strategies that we will cover in this book are spreads, straddles and strangles. In this chapter we will be looking at option spreads. Straddles and strangles are covered in chapter 15.

Multiple option strategies

As we have already covered so far, there are four basic strategies you can employ when trading options:

⇨ buying call options

⇨ buying put options

⇨ selling call options

⇨ selling put options.

You can combine these four basic strategies to achieve a number of different strategies. For example, long and short option positions can be used in combination so that their risks offset each other. Some of these strategies are designed so that you will profit if the market moves in either direction. Other strategies are designed to limit your risk, and some will create profits if the stock price remains within a specific range.

When you consider any option strategies, it is important to consider the underlying stock. It is the movement in price of the underlying stock that will determine the effectiveness of your option strategy. It is easy to be lured by the high returns on options and forget to properly analyse the underlying stock to ensure it is appropriate for your strategy.

It is also important to consider your transaction costs when considering multiple option strategies. You will be incurring entry and exit fees on multiple option contracts, and potentially stock purchase as well, so you need to factor these costs into your profit analysis to determine the profitability of your strategy.

Option spread strategies

A spread strategy is when you open both a long position and a short position in options over the same underlying stock. To be a spread, the options must have different strike prices, different expiration dates or both. The spread increases the potential profit that you can make on the trade and can also reduce your risk in the event of a significant market movement.

Spreads are used to take advantage of the time value in options, which deteriorates as the options approach expiry. Your advantage comes through offsetting long and short positions. Generally, a short-term spread strategy will involve one option that is at-the-money or in-the-money and one that is out-of-the-money. The options will change in value at different rates, due to the presence of intrinsic value in one option only.

Some of the more common spread strategies that we will discuss are:

⇨ bull spread

⇨ bull put spread

⇨ bear spread

⇨ bear call spread

⇨ ratio call spread

⇨ calendar spread.

Bull spread

A bull spread is a strategy you might use if you are speculating that the market value of the underlying stock will rise (that is, you are bullish on the stock) but you also feel that the price increase will be limited. You want to benefit from the price increase but also wish to reduce your cost of buying a call option over the stock.

The bull spread strategy involves buying a call option and selling a call option that has a higher strike price. It is a strategy with limited risk and limited reward. Your maximum profit is the difference between the strike prices of the two options, less the net premium you paid for setting up the spread. The total risk of this strategy is the net cost to enter the two option positions. This loss will be incurred if the market value of the underlying stock remains below the strike price of your bought option.

The selling of the higher strike price call option provides premium revenue to offset the cost of your bought call option. This reduces the overall risk on your trade and it reduces your total cost to enter, but also increases your transaction costs.

Although you are selling an uncovered call option, your risk is limited as you have bought a call option with a lower strike price that you can exercise if your uncovered call option is exercised.

A bull spread is an example of a vertical spread, as you are buying and selling options with different strike prices but the same expiry date. This is shown in figure 14.1.

Figure 14.1: vertical spread diagram

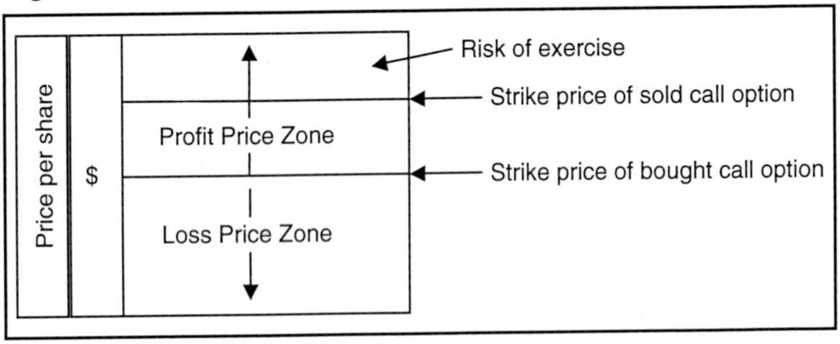

Tip

A bull spread strategy will be most profitable when the market value of the underlying stock moves to or above the strike price of your sold call option.

We look at the use of a bull spread in example 14.1.

Example 14.1

You have been watching the price of ANZ shares, which are currently trading at $21.90. You believe they will increase up to around $24.00 but no further in the next three months.

You decide to enter a bull spread on ANZ and buy five $22.00 call options for $0.90 and sell five $24.00 call options for $0.20.

Over the next few months, the market value of ANZ moves as you expected to $23.90. Your bought calls are now in-the-money and worth $1.95 and your sold call options are valued at $0.05.

You decide to close out both option positions as you are close to your maximum profit and would rather avoid exercise on your sold options.

Cost to buy call options*	($450.00)
Proceeds on sale of options*	$100.00
Net cost of option spread*	($350.00)
Proceeds on sale of options*	$975.00
Cost to close sold option position*	($25.00)
Net proceeds on closing your spread*	$950.00
Total return on the trade*	$600.00

* Does not include transaction costs.

Example 14.1 is close to the best case scenario. If the market value of ANZ had remained below the strike price of your bought options of $22, both of your options would have expired worthless and your net loss on the transaction would be $350 (your cost to enter).

Once the price of ANZ rises above $22, your bought option will gain intrinsic value. You need the value of your bought option to increase enough to offset the cost of entering the spread in order to generate a profit.

If the price of ANZ rose sharply above the strike price of your sold option, you will be at risk of exercise. This can be offset by closing your option positions. Alternatively, if your sold option is exercised, you would exercise your bought option so you can deliver the underlying shares.

In example 14.2 we outline the same bull spread scenario as in example 14.1, but the value of the underlying share price rises above your expectations.

Example 14.2

You have been watching the price of ANZ shares, which are currently trading at $21.90. You believe they will increase up to around $24.00 but no further in the next three months.

You decide to enter a bull spread on ANZ and buy five $22.00 call options for $0.90 and sell five $24.00 call options for $0.20.

Over the next few months, the market value of ANZ rises sharply to $26.00. Your bought call options are now in-the-money and worth $4.20. Your sold call options are also in-the-money and valued at $2.20.

You decide to close out both option positions to avoid exercise.

Cost to buy call options*	($450.00)
Proceeds on sale of options*	$100.00
Net cost of option spread*	($350.00)
Proceeds on sale of options*	$2 100.00
Cost to close sold option position*	($1 100.00)
Net proceeds on closing your spread*	$1 000.00
Total return on the trade*	$650.00

* Does not include transaction costs.

It is important to note that in example 14.2 your sold call options may have been exercised at any time they were in-the-money before you closed your position. Even though the market value of ANZ rose sharply, you profit is still limited to the spread.

Summary for the bull spread strategy

The following list is a summary of the key points when considering a bull spread strategy.

⇨ It is a limited risk and limited reward strategy.

⇨ It is cheaper than buying a call option in isolation but incurs higher transaction costs.

⇨ Consider this strategy when you are expecting a limited increase in the market price of the underlying stock.

⇨ Always ensure the cost to enter the spread is worth the potential reward.

⇨ You must enter and exit both options at the same time.

Bull put spread

You can also construct a bull spread strategy using put options instead of call options. A bull put spread involves selling a put option and buying a put option with a lower strike price. In this case you are speculating that the price of the underlying stock will remain above the strike price of your sold put option (so that you retain the option premium); however, you buy a lower priced put option to provide you with downside protection in case the market value of the underlying stock falls sharply.

In this strategy, your profit is limited to the net premium you receive on selling your put and buying the lower strike price put. Your losses are limited to the difference in the strike prices of the options less the net premium you received.

The disadvantage of this strategy is that you are at a higher risk of your written option being exercised as your written put is closer to being in-the-money. You also need to provide a margin to cover your written puts as they are at a higher strike price than your bought puts. Example 14.3 (overleaf) illustrates the use of a bull put strategy.

Example 14.3

You have been watching the price of ANZ shares, which are currently trading at $21.90. You believe they will remain above $21.00 over the next three months.

You decide to enter a bull put spread on ANZ and sell 10 $20.50 put options for $0.50 and buy 10 $19.50 put options for $0.10.

Over the next few months, the market value of ANZ stays above $21.00 as expected and your options expire worthless.

Cost to buy put options*	($100.00)
Proceeds on sale of options*	$500.00
Net proceeds of option spread*	$400.00

* Does not include transaction costs.

Example 14.3 is the best case scenario for a bull put spread strategy. The situation would be different if the market value of the underlying stock fell below the strike price of your sold put option. In example 14.4, we illustrate this situation.

Example 14.4

You have been watching the price of ANZ shares, which are currently trading at $21.90. You believe they will remain above $21.00 over the next three months.

You decide to enter a bull put spread on ANZ and sell 10 $20.50 put options for $0.50 and buy 10 $19.50 put options for $0.10.

Over the next few months, the market value of ANZ falls to $20.00. Your written put options are in-the-money and valued at $0.60. Your bought put options are out-of-the-money and valued at $0.10.

You decide to close out both option positions to avoid exercise.

Cost to buy put options*	($100.00)
Proceeds on sale of options*	$500.00

Net proceeds of option spread*	$400.00
Proceeds on sale of options*	$100.00
Cost to close sold option position*	($600.00)
Net cost on closing your spread*	($500.00)
Total loss on the trade*	($100.00)
* Does not include transaction costs.	

The total risk for a bull put strategy is the difference in the strike prices less the net premium you received on opening the spread. So, if in example 14.4 the price of ANZ fell below $19.50, the total loss would be $600.00 (i.e. the spread of $1.00, totalling $1000.00, less the net proceeds on opening of $400.00).

Bear spreads

A bear spread strategy works in a similar fashion to the bull spread strategy, except that you are speculating on a moderate fall in the market value of the underlying stock. You want to benefit from the price decrease but also wish to reduce your cost of buying a put option over the stock.

The bear spread strategy involves buying an at-the-money put option and selling an out-of-the-money put option that has a lower strike price. As with the bull spread, this is a strategy with limited risk and limited reward. Your maximum profit is the difference between the strike prices of the two options, less the net premium you paid for setting up the spread. This will be achieved if the market value of the underlying stock falls to the strike price of your sold put option. The total risk of this strategy is the net cost to enter the two option positions. This risk will eventuate if the market value of the underlying stock remains above the strike price of your bought option. A bear spread is shown in figure 14.2 (overleaf).

Figure 14.2: example of a bear spread

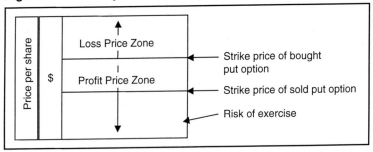

Tip

A bear spread strategy will be most profitable when the market value of the underlying stock moves down to or below the strike price of your sold put option.

In example 14.5, we look at the use of the bear spread strategy to profit on a moderate fall in value of ANZ.

Example 14.5

You have been watching the price of ANZ shares, which are currently trading at $21.90. You believe they will fall to around $19.00 but no further in the next three months.

You decide to enter a bear spread on ANZ and buy 10 $21.00 put options for $0.45 and sell 10 $19.00 put options for $0.15.

A few days before expiry, the market value of ANZ moves as you expected down to $19.00. Your bought puts are now in-the-money and worth $2.00 and your sold put options are valued at $0.05.

You decide to close out both option positions as you are close to your maximum profit and would rather avoid exercise on your sold options.

Cost to buy put options*	($450.00)
Proceeds on sale of options*	$150.00

Net cost of option spread*	($300.00)
Proceeds on sale of options*	$2 000.00
Cost to close sold option position*	($50.00)
Net proceeds on closing your spread*	$1 950.00
Total return on the trade*	$1 650.00
* Does not include transaction costs.	

Example 14.5 is close to the best case scenario. Once the price of ANZ fell below $21.00, your bought option gained intrinsic value.

If the market value of ANZ had remained above the strike price of your bought put options of $21.00, both of your options would have expired worthless and your net loss on the transaction would have been $300 (your cost to enter).

If the price of ANZ fell sharply below the strike price of your sold option, you would have been at risk of exercise. This can be offset by closing your option positions. If your sold option is exercised, you would need to purchase the ANZ shares at $20.00. You would then exercise your bought option to on-sell the underlying shares at $21.00.

To profit from a bear spread strategy you need the value of your bought option to increase by more than the cost of entering the spread.

Summary for the bear spread strategy

The following list is a summary of the key points when considering a bear spread strategy.

⇨ It is a limited risk and limited reward strategy.

⇨ It is cheaper than buying a put option in isolation but incurs higher transaction costs.

⇨ Consider this strategy when you are expecting a limited decrease in the market price of the underlying stock.

⇨ Always ensure the cost to enter the spread is worth the potential reward.

⇨ You must enter and exit both options at the same time.

Bear call spread

You can also construct a bear spread strategy using call options instead of put options. A bear call spread involves selling a call option and buying a call option with a higher strike price. In this case you are speculating that the price of the underlying stock will remain below the strike price of your sold call option (so that you retain the option premium); however, you buy a higher strike price call option to provide you with upside protection in case the market value of the underlying stock rises sharply.

In this strategy, your profit is limited to the net premium you receive on selling your call option and buying the higher strike price call. Your losses are limited to the difference in the strike prices of the options less the net premium you received.

The disadvantage of this strategy, like the bull put spread, is that you are at a higher risk of your written option being exercised as your written call is closer to being in-the-money. Any increase in the market value of the underlying stock may result in early exercise of your written call option. You also need to provide a margin to cover your written calls as they are at a lower strike price than your bought calls.

In example 14.6, we illustrate the use of the bear call spread strategy and the value of effective management of your option positions.

Example 14.6

You have been watching the price of ANZ shares, which are currently trading at $21.90. You believe they will remain below $23.00 over the next three months.

You decide to enter a bear call spread on ANZ and sell 10 $23.00 call options for $0.45 and buy 10 $25.00 call options for $0.05.

Over the next few months, the market value of ANZ moves to $23.20. Your sold calls are now in-the-money and priced at $0.25. Your bought call options are still priced at $0.05. You decide to close your spread position.

Cost to buy call options*	($50.00)
Proceeds on sale of call options*	$450.00
Net proceeds of option spread*	$400.00
Cost to close sold call options*	($250.00)
Proceeds on sale of bought call options*	$50.00
Net cost to close option spread*	($200.00)
Net profit on total transaction*	$200.00

* Does not include transaction costs.

Example 14.6 shows how you can still realise a profit on this spread when the market moves against you if you exit early. However, your transaction costs may have used up much of this profit.

Ratio call spread

The ratio call spread is a strategy you might use to speculate on a slight rise in the market, but you are also concerned that the market may then experience a fall in prices.

The ratio call spread involves the purchase of a call option and the sale of multiple call options with a higher strike price. Ideally, you would open the spread at a profit—so that the premiums on the sold calls were greater than the premium on your bought call. However, this may not always be the case. If the price moves above the strike price of your bought call, it will appreciate in value and earn you a profit. However, you do not want the market value of the underlying stock to move above the strike price of your sold options, as this will put you at risk of exercise and potential losses.

A ratio call spread is shown in figure 14.3.

Figure 14.3: example of a ratio call spread

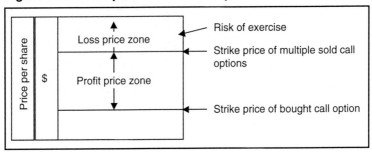

Your maximum profit will be achieved when the market value of the underlying stock is at the strike price of your sold call options. This returns you the maximum value on your bought options without creating a loss on your sold call options.

If the market value of the underlying stock moves or remains below the strike price of your bought option, your net profit or loss will be the net profit or cost to open the spread.

The ratio of bought calls to sold calls is generally 1:2. This places the trader at risk of losses if the market value of the underlying stock rises strongly above the strike price of the sold call options. You only have one bought option to cover one sold option. The additional sold options are uncovered calls and carry the risk of unlimited losses in the event of a significant rise in market value of the underlying stock. The higher the ratio of sold calls, the greater this risk will be.

Tip

You will need to provide margin for the uncovered call positions.

Example 14.7 shows the use of the ratio call spread strategy.

Example 14.7

You have been watching the price of WES shares, which have recently risen to $31.50. You believe they might increase a little further, but are also at risk of a retracement after the recent rise.

You decide to enter a ratio call spread on WES and buy five $32.00 call options for $1.00 and sell 10 $33.00 call options for $0.65 each.

Cost to buy call option*	($500.00)
Proceeds on sale of options*	$650.00
Net profit on opening option spread*	$150.00

* Does not include transaction costs.

In example 14.7 you have created a net return on opening your option spread. If the market value of WES falls and remains below $32.00, you will retain this profit as all options will expire worthless.

In example 14.8, we consider the outcome of the same ratio call spread strategy of example 14.7 when the market moves as you expect.

Example 14.8

Over the next month, the market value of WES moves up to $32.80. Your bought calls are now in-the-money and worth $1.50 and your sold call options are valued at $0.35. You decide to close your option spread to avoid exercise on your sold options.

Net profit on opening option spread*	$150.00
Proceeds on sale of options*	$750.00
Cost to close sold option positions*	($350.00)
Net proceeds on closing your spread*	$400.00

Example 14.8 *(cont'd)*

Total return on the trade* $550.00

* Does not include transaction costs.

In example 14.8 you decided to close your option spread and generated a net profit before $550 before transaction costs.

In example 14.9, we look at the same ratio call spread over WES, but consider the outcome if the market value of WES experiences a sharp increase so that your sold option moves into the money.

Example 14.9

Over the next month, the market value of WES moves up to $32.80. Your bought calls are now in-the-money and worth $1.50 and your sold call options are valued at $0.35. You decide to keep your spread open to further increase your profit through time decay on your sold options.

However, the price of WES jumps up to $34.00 on some unexpected news. Your bought option is now worth $2.60 and your sold options are now in-the-money and worth $1.60. You quickly close your spread to prevent further loss.

Net profit on opening option spread*	$150.00
Proceeds on sale of options*	$1 300.00
Cost to close sold option positions*	($1 600.00)
Net proceeds on closing your spread*	($300.00)
Total return on the trade*	($150.00)

* Does not include transaction costs.

Example 14.9 shows how your profits can very quickly become losses on a ratio call spread if the market value of the underlying stock rises above the strike price of your sold call options. As the price rises above this point, the cost to close the sold options increases twice as fast as the price you receive on your bought option as your ratio is 1:2 (you have five bought options and 10 sold options).

Summary for the ratio call spread strategy

The following list is a summary of the key points when considering a ratio call spread strategy.

⇨ Consider this strategy when you are expecting a limited increase in the market price of the underlying stock and may be concerned about a sell-off.

⇨ It is a limited reward strategy — profit is limited to the difference in the strike prices of your options, plus your net profit/cost on opening the spread.

⇨ Ideally, you open the spread with a net profit.

⇨ Your net profit or cost if the market price falls is the net profit/cost to open the spread.

⇨ It offers unlimited risk on uncovered call options. Be prepared to close your positions if the market price of the underlying stock moves up strongly.

⇨ It is cheaper than buying a call option in isolation but incurs higher transaction costs.

⇨ Always ensure the cost to enter the spread is worth the potential reward.

⇨ You must enter and exit both options at the same time.

Calendar spread

The calendar spread is another variation of the spread strategy that involves options with the same strike price but different expiry dates. This strategy allows you to generate a profit from time decay when the market price of the underlying stock is trading within a stable range. It is also achieved without the risk of having an uncovered call option, or the need to own the underlying stock.

The calendar spread strategy involves selling a call with a close expiry date and buying a call at the same strike price but with a longer time to expiry. Your ideal outcome is that the market value of the underlying stock is at-the-money when your first option expires. You will retain the option premium on your sold option, and close your long dated option while it still has time value remaining. Your profit is generated as the time decay on your close dated option will be faster than the time decay on your long dated option.

If the market value of the underlying stock moves above your strike price, your option is at risk of exercise. Even though you have your long dated option to hedge against this event, this is not your desired outcome due to the cost and effort involved in exercise of the options. If this occurs, you need to decide to either close your position or hold if you feel the market price will fall back below the strike price in the near term.

If the market value of the underlying stock falls dramatically, you may consider either closing your spread early so that you do not lose too much time value in your bought option or holding if you feel the market price will rebound.

Example 14.10 illustrates a calendar spread strategy over TLS.

Example 14.10

You have been watching the price of TLS and believe it will remain at or below $3.00. It is currently trading at $2.95.

You decide to open a calendar spread by selling 100 one-month $3 calls for two and a half cents, and buying 100 three-month $3 calls for $0.05.

Cost of bought options*	$500.00
Proceeds on sale of options*	$250.00
Net cost on opening your spread*	($250.00)

One month later, on expiry of your bought options, TLS is trading at $2.96. Your sold options expire worthless, and your bought options are now worth four and a half cents. You close your bought options.

Proceeds on sale of options* $450.00

Net profit on the calendar spread* $200.00

* Does not include transaction costs.

Summary for the calendar spread strategy

Following is a summary of the key points when considering a calendar spread strategy.

⇨ Consider this strategy when you are expecting the market price to remain flat within a stable trading range.

⇨ Profit is generated on the different speeds of time decay on the two options.

⇨ You need to close your long dated call on expiry of the first call option otherwise your strategy has changed.

⇨ Be prepared to close your positions if the market price of the underlying stock moves up strongly and you want to avoid exercise.

⇨ You should also consider closing both option positions if the market value of the underlying stock falls significantly.

Chapter summary

⇨ The four basic option strategies are buying calls, buying puts, selling calls and selling puts.

⇨ You can combine the four basic strategies to achieve a number of different strategies.

⇨ Ensure you carefully consider the value and potential price movement of the underlying stock in any option strategy.

⇨ When using combined option strategies, you need to be mindful of your transactions costs as these will increase with the number of options involved.

⇨ Option spread strategies involve opening a long position and a short position over the same underlying stock. The options will have different strike prices, different expiry dates or both.

⇨ Types of option spread strategies include:

- ✠ bull spread
- ✠ bull put spread
- ✠ bear spread
- ✠ bear call spread
- ✠ ratio call spread
- ✠ calendar spread.

⇨ Many multiple option positions involve selling options so that risk of exercise must be considered. Early exercise of an option can considerably affect the outcome of your strategy.

⇨ Potential for profit and risk are interrelated. Option strategies with the potential for large profits will also carry higher risks that need to be assessed and managed.

⇨ With multiple option strategies, ensure you close all option positions simultaneously otherwise you will be changing your strategy.

⇨ Ensure you fully understand any option strategy you wish to open.

chapter 15

Advanced strategies: straddles and strangles

In this chapter we will look at two other types of multiple option strategies. These are straddles and strangles.

Option straddle strategy

Straddle strategies involve buying or selling options with the same strike price and the same expiry date. When buying put and call options simultaneously, you are opening a long straddle.

The long straddle strategy is designed to create a profit if the market value of the underlying stock moves significantly. It is often used when a stock has been trading in a stable trading range and you are speculating that the price will break out in the near term. It is also appropriate for volatile stocks, although the cost to open the position will be higher on these stocks.

The short straddle strategy involves selling put and call options with the same strike price and the same expiry date. This is designed to create a profit if the market value of the underlying stock remains stable. This is a much higher risk strategy as you have two uncovered option positions.

Long straddle strategy

A long straddle strategy involves buying the same number of call options and put options with the same strike price and the same expiry date. To open a long straddle, you need to be speculating that the market value of the underlying stock will move dramatically within the life of your options.

As you are buying both call options and put options, the cost of these options is the cost to open your straddle position. This is the maximum risk you have for this strategy.

If the market value of the underlying stock moves up sharply, your call option will be in-the-money and its value will increase. If the market value of the underlying stock moves down, your put option will be in-the-money and its value will increase. The increase in your in-the-money option needs to be significant enough to offset the cost of entering your straddle for you to generate a profit on this strategy.

Tip

The higher the cost of your options, the more the stock price needs to move for you to make a profit on a straddle position.

A long straddle strategy using CBA options is illustrated in example 15.1.

Example 15.1

You have been watching the price of CBA, whaich has been trading between $52.00 and $53.00. You believe it will shortly break out into a new trend but you are not sure in which direction. It is currently trading at $52.50.

You decide to open a long straddle by buying five $52.50 call options for $0.45 and buying five $52.50 put options for $0.80.

Cost of call options*	$225.00
Cost of put options*	$400.00
Net cost on opening your straddle*	$625.00

* Does not include transaction costs.

In example 15.1 you will need the market value of the underlying stock to move enough to create an increase in value on either your puts or calls of at least $625.00 to break even on your straddle position. This requires the price of CBA to move by at least $1.25 (the cost of your options) from your strike price of $52.50.

In example 15.2, we look at the outcome of our long straddle from example 15.1 when the market value of CBA falls significantly.

Example 15.2

One month later the price of CBA has broken down and is now trading at $49.50. Your call options are worth only $0.01 and your put options are now worth $3.10. You feel that the price is due to retrace upward and wish to take your profits. You sell your put options and, given the cost of selling your call options, decide to let them expire worthless.

Proceeds on sale of options*	$1 550.00
Net profit on the straddle*	$200.00

* Does not include transaction costs.

It is important to analyse the movement in price of the underlying stock to time your exit for maximum profit. If the price moves significantly and you decide to hold the position open, you face the risk of the price reversing and losing the profit on your straddle.

Summary for the long straddle strategy

The following list contains a summary of the key points to consider for a long straddle strategy.

⇨ Consider this strategy when you are expecting the market price of the underlying stock to break out of a trading range, but you are not sure in which direction the price will move.

⇨ Profit is generated on the straddle if the movement in the underlying stock price is more than the combined cost of your options.

⇨ Your risk on a straddle is your cost to open the option positions.

⇨ Select an expiry date that gives you enough time for your strategy to work.

⇨ Be prepared to close your positions if the market price of the underlying stock moves up or down strongly to maximise your profit.

Short straddle strategy

A short straddle strategy involves selling the same number of call options and put options with the same strike price and the same expiry date. To open a short straddle, you need to be speculating that the market value of the underlying stock will remain within a small trading range that is less than the premium you receive on selling both options.

As you are selling both call options and put options, the premium on these options is your maximum profit. You are looking for time decay to work in your favour and for the options to expire worthless. You will also be required to provide margin for both your positions.

If the market value of the underlying stock moves significantly in either direction, you are at risk of significant losses. This strategy involves selling uncovered calls and puts, creating potentially large losses in both directions.

You will generate a profit on this strategy if the market price of the underlying stock moves by less than the combined premium on your options. However, you are at risk of exercise at all times either option is in-the-money. The aim is that if the market value of the stock remains stable, exercise is unlikely as the cost to exercise will outweigh the small benefit to the option buyer.

Example 15.3 illustrates the use of a short straddle strategy using TLS options.

Example 15.3

You have been watching the price of TLS, which has been trading within $0.10 either side of $2.95. You do not expect this to change.

You decide to open a short straddle by selling 50 $2.95 call options for $0.05 and selling five $2.95 put options for $0.15.

Premium on call options*	$250.00
Premium on put options*	$750.00
Total premium on opening your straddle*	$1 000.00

* Does not include transaction costs.

In example 15.3, if the market price of TLS moves by less than $0.20 from $2.95 and your options are not exercised, you will keep the premium of $1000.00 as profit (before transaction costs).

Summary for the short straddle strategy

The following list contains a summary of the key points to consider for a short straddle strategy.

⇨ Consider this strategy when you are expecting the market price of the underlying stock to remain within a tight trading range.

⇨ Profit is generated on the straddle from time decay on your sold options.

⇨ You will need to provide margin for both your sold option positions.

⇨ Your risk on a straddle can be large if the market value of the underlying stock moves significantly.

⇨ You are at risk of exercise whenever either option is in-the-money.

⇨ Select an expiry date that provides enough time value in your option but keeps the risk of a large movement in the underlying stock price to a reasonable level.

⇨ Be prepared to close your positions if the market price of the underlying stock moves up or down strongly.

Option strangle strategies

An option strangle strategy combines the features of both the spread and the straddle strategies. There are two main types of strangle strategies that involve either buying or selling out-of-the-money options.

The long strangle strategy involves buying put and call options and relies on a significant movement in the price of the underlying stock to generate a profit. This is less expensive to open than a long straddle strategy, but requires a larger movement in the price of the underlying stock to generate a profit.

The short strangle strategy involves selling put and call options and is used to speculate that the price of the underlying stock will remain between the strike prices of the options. Your profit on a short strangle strategy will be less than for a similar short straddle strategy, but your risk is also lower.

Long strangle strategy

The long strangle strategy involves buying a call option with a higher strike price and buying a put option with a lower strike price than the current market price of the underlying stock. The premiums to buy both of these options will be out-of-the-money, making this strategy less expensive than a straddle strategy.

However, as both options are out-of-the-money, the price of the underlying stock needs to move a further distance in order to create intrinsic value in one of the options so that you can generate a profit on the strategy.

You need to be speculating that the price of the underlying stock is about to undergo a dramatic move in either direction (but you don't know if it will be up or down). You need the price of the underlying stock to move far enough beyond the strike price of one of your options to offset the cost of opening the strangle and create a profit.

Time decay is a significant issue in a strangle strategy. As both options are out-of-the-money, they consist solely of time value. It is best to close your option positions well before expiry to reduce the impact of time decay on the value of your options.

Example 15.4 illustrates the use of a long strangle strategy using CBA options.

Example 15.4

You have been watching the price of CBA, which has been trading between $52.00 and $53.00. You believe it will shortly break out into a new trend but you are not sure in which direction. It is currently trading at $52.50.

You decide to open a long strangle by buying five $53.00 call options for $0.80 and buying five $52.00 put options for $0.55.

Cost of call options*	$400.00
Cost of put options*	$275.00
Net cost on opening your straddle*	$675.00

* Does not include transaction costs.

In example 15.4 you need the price of CBA to move by more than $1.32 (cost of your options) either above $53.00 or below $52.00 to generate a profit on your straddle at expiry. You will need less of a movement if the price of CBA moves significantly before expiry as your options will still have some time value remaining in their premium.

Summary for the long strangle strategy

The following list contains a summary of the key points to consider for a long strangle strategy.

⇨ Consider this strategy when you are expecting the market price of the underlying stock to break out of a trading range and have a significant price movement.

⇨ Profit is generated on a long strangle if the movement in the underlying stock price is more than the combined cost of your options beyond the strike price of the in-the-money option.

⇨ Your risk on a long strangle is your cost to open the option positions.

⇨ Select an expiry date that gives you enough time for your strategy to work.

⇨ It is best to close your long strangle well before expiry to maximise any remaining time value on your options.

⇨ Be prepared to close your positions if the market price of the underlying stock moves up or down strongly to maximise your profit.

Short strangle strategy

The short strangle strategy involves selling an out-of-the-money call option with a higher strike price and selling a put option with a lower strike price than the current market price of the underlying stock. The premiums on selling both of these options represent your maximum profit potential from this strategy.

Your premiums received on the short strangle will be lower than for a straddle as you are selling out-of-the-money options. However, your risk is also lower as the stock price has more room to move before your options move into the money.

As you are opening an uncovered call option and a put option, you will be required to provide margin for both of these positions. This cost should also be factored into your profit analysis.

You are speculating that the price of the underlying stock will remain below the strike price of your call option and above the strike price of your put option. In this case, both options will remain out-of-the-money and you will keep the option premiums as profit on your short strangle.

However, if the market value of the underlying stock moves beyond either strike price, you are at risk of exercise and your losses can potentially be significant.

We use CBA options to illustrate the short strangle strategy in example 15.5.

Example 15.5

You have been watching the price of CBA, which has been trading between $52.00 and $53.00. You believe it will remain within this range.

You decide to open a short strangle by selling five $53.00 call options for $0.80 and selling five $52.00 put options for $0.55.

Premium on call options*	$400.00
Premium on put options*	$275.00
Total premium on opening your straddle*	$675.00

* Does not include transaction costs.

In example 15.5, as long as the price of CBA does not move either above $53.00 or below $52.00 before expiry, your options will expire worthless and you will retain the option premium. If the market value of CBA moves sharply towards either strike price, you may consider closing your strangle to avoid the risk of the option moving into the money and potential exercise.

Summary for the short strangle strategy

The following list contains a summary of the key points to consider for a short strangle strategy.

⇨ Consider this strategy when you are expecting the market price of the underlying stock to remain within a specific trading range.

⇨ Profit is generated from the time decay on your option premiums.

⇨ Your maximum profit is achieved if the market price of the underlying stock remains between the strike prices of your options and your options expire worthless.

⇨ Your risk on a short strangle is significant if either option moves into the money.

⇨ Select an expiry date that gives you enough time value in your options but limits the opportunity for the underlying stock price to move significantly before expiry.

⇨ Consider closing your short strangle if your option is at risk of moving into the money and therefore might be at risk of exercise.

Chapter summary

⇨ Option straddles involve buying or selling put and call options with the same strike price and the same expiry date.

⇨ A long option straddle involves buying the same number of call options and put options with the same strike price and the same expiry date.

⇨ You will profit on a long option straddle if the market value of the underlying stock moves significantly in either direction.

⇨ A short option straddle involves selling the same number of call options and put options with the same strike price and the same expiry date.

⇨ A short option straddle is a high risk strategy as you are exposed to risk for any movement in the underlying stock.

⇨ You will profit on a short option straddle if the market value of the underlying stock remains stable.

⇨ Option strangles combine the features of an option spread and an option straddle.

⇨ A long option strangle involves buying out-of-the-money call and put options with the same expiry.

⇨ A long option strangle is less expensive to open than a long straddle, but requires a larger movement in the underlying stock to generate a profit.

⇨ A short strangle involves selling out-of-the-money put and call options with the same expiry date.

⇨ Premiums received on a short strangle are lower than for a short straddle; however, the risk of this strategy is also lower.

⇨ Potential for profit and risk are interrelated. Option strategies with the potential for large profits will also carry higher risks that need to be assessed and managed.

⇨ With multiple option strategies, ensure you close all option positions simultaneously, otherwise you will be changing your strategy.

⇨ Ensure you fully understand any option strategy you wish to open.

Appendix

Table A1 provides a summary of the option strategies we have discussed. For each strategy, we list the risk involved and profit potential. We also indicate when this strategy might be appropriate based on your view of the market value of the underlying stock.

Table A1: summary of option strategies

Option strategy	Market view	Risk	Profit potential
Buying call options	*Bullish* Speculating on a rise in the market value of the underlying stock	Option premium paid	Unlimited
Buying put options	*Bearish* Speculating on a fall in the market value of the underlying stock	Option premium paid	Significant; limited to the market value of the underlying stock at the strike price of the option
Selling covered call options	*Stable or slightly bearish* Speculating that the market value of the underlying stock will remain flat or fall	Options will be exercised and underlying shares will need to be sold at the strike price	Premium received

Table A1: summary of option strategies (cont'd)

Option strategy	Market view	Risk	Profit potential
Selling naked call options	*Stable or slightly bearish* Speculating that the market value of the underlying stock will remain flat or fall	Potentially unlimited	Premium received
Selling put options	*Stable or slightly bullish* Speculating that the market value of the underlying stock will remain flat or rise	Significant; potentially the value of the underlying stock at the strike price, less premium received	Premium received
Bull spreads *Buy a call option and sell a call option with a higher strike price*	*Slightly bullish* Speculating on a small or moderate rise in the market value of the underlying stock	Net premium paid	Difference between the strike prices of the two options less the net premium paid
Bull put spreads *Sell a put option and buy a put option with a lower strike price*	*Stable or slightly bullish* Speculating the market value of the underlying stock will remain above the strike price of your sold option	Difference between the strike prices of the two options less the net premium received	Net premium received
Bear spreads *Buy an at-the-money put option and sell a put option with a lower strike price*	*Slightly bearish* Speculating the market value of the underlying stock will fall to the strike price of your sold option	Net premium paid	Difference between the strike prices of the two options, less the net premium paid

Option strategy	Market view	Risk	Profit potential
Bear call spread *Sell a call option and buy a call option with a higher strike price*	*Stable or slightly bearish* Speculating the market value of the underlying stock will remain below the strike price of your sold option	Difference between the strike prices of the two options, less the net premium received	Net premium received
Ratio call spread *Buy a call option and sell multiple call options with a higher strike price*	*Slightly bullish* Speculating the market value of the underlying stock will rise but not above the strike price of your sold call options	Potentially unlimited if a significant rise in market value of the underlying stock	Value of your bought call option at the strike price of the sold options, plus the net premium received/paid to open the spread
Calendar spread *Sell a call option and buy a call option with the same strike price but a later expiry date*	*Stable* Speculating the market value of the underlying stock will remain at-the-money to expiry	Net cost to open the spread	Net proceeds to close the spread, less net cost to open the spread
Long straddle *Buy call options and put options with the same strike price and same expiry*	*Expecting significant movement in either direction*	Net cost to open the straddle	Increase in value of the in-the-money option less cost to open the long straddle
Short straddle *Sell call options and put options with the same strike price and same expiry date*	*Stable* Speculating the market value of the underlying stock will remain at or near the strike price of the options	Potentially unlimited	Total premium received to open the short straddle

Table A1: summary of option strategies (cont'd)

Option strategy	Market view	Risk	Profit potential
Long strangle *Buy an out-of-the-money call option and out-of-the-money put option*	*Expecting significant movement in either direction*	Net cost to open the strangle	Increase in value of the in-the-money option less cost to open the long strangle
Short strangle *Sell an out-of-the-money call option and an out-of-the-money put option*	*Stable* Speculating the market value of the underlying stock will remain between the strike prices of your options	Potentially unlimited	Total premium received to open the short strangle

Glossary

American style options A type of option contract that allows the holder to exercise the option at any time up to and including the day of expiry.

ask price The price quoted on the ASX as the price at which a seller is offering to sell a security or derivative.

assignment The allocation by ASX Clear of exercise of a specific option to a randomly selected seller of the same type of option.

at-the-money options Options whereby the market value of the underlying stock is the same as the strike price of the option.

auto-exercise An option your broker may offer whereby any in-the-money options you hold with be automatically exercised on expiry.

bid price The price quoted on the ASX as the price at which a buyer is offering to buy a security or derivative.

cash settled A process on exercise of index options that involves settlement of all in-the-money options at their cash value.

combination order An order that simultaneously effects a buy and sell order that allows you to roll over an option position, usually to a later expiry date.

company issued options Options that are issued directly by a company and not listed on the ASX.

covered call options The sale of call options whereby the seller also owns the underlying stock and this stock is lodged as margin for the option position.

daily volatility The usually intraday movement in price of a stock.

European style options A type of option contract that only allows the holder to exercise their option on the expiry date.

exercise The holder of an option elects to enforce their rights to either buy or sell the underlying stock at the strike price of their option.

expiry date The date on which an option no longer affords any rights to the holder and ceases to exist. Actual expiry for stock options occurs at the close of trade on the expiry date.

fundamental analysis A process of analysing stocks that refers to fundamental information about the company, including items such as net assets, earnings, projected earnings, dividends, and economic and industrial factors.

hedging Entering a transaction that reduces or offsets your risk in a current holding.

index multiplier A value that is used to convert point value of an index or index option into a dollar value.

index options Options issued over a stock index.

in-the-money When an option holds intrinsic value.

intrinsic value The value of an option represented by the distance between the strike price of the option and current market value of the underlying stock.

limit order An order to buy or sell a security or derivative at a set price.

margins The security that an option writer must provide to ASX Clear to ensure they can meet their obligations under the option.

market order An order to buy or sell a security or derivative at the current market price quoted on the ASX.

naked call options The sale of call options whereby the seller does not own the underlying stock. Also referred to as uncovered call options.

open interest The total number of open contracts in a particular type of option.

open position Any option contract that you have sold or bought that has not been closed, exercised or expired.

opening purchase The purchase of an option that creates an open option position for the buyer.

opening sale The sale of an option that creates an open option position for the seller.

out-of-the-money When an option holds no intrinsic value.

pay-off diagram A diagram that illustrates the break-even point for an option position at expiry (when the option no longer holds any time value).

premium The amount paid to buy or the amount received on sale of an option.

premium margin The component of the margin provided by an option seller that represents the current premium value of the option.

risk margin The component of the margin provided by an option seller that represents the expected volatility in the value of the option.

short selling A strategy that involves selling a security first and buying it back later with a view to creating a profit from an expected fall in value of the security.

spreads Option strategies that involve opening both a long position and a short position in options over the same underlying stock. To be a spread, the options must have different strike prices, different expiration dates or both.

straddles Option strategies that involve simultaneously buying and selling options with the same strike price and the same expiry.

strangles Option strategies that involve simultaneously buying and selling options with different strike prices but the same expiry.

strike price The price at which the option holder can either sell or buy the underlying stock if they choose to exercise the option.

taker The person who buys an option to create an open option position.

technical analysis A process of analysis that uses price charts to form a view on the future price movements of a stock.

time value The component of an option premium that represents the potential for the option value to increase.

uncovered calls The sale of call options whereby the seller does not own the underlying stock. Also referred to as naked call options.

vertical spread A spread strategy whereby you buy and sell options with the same expiry date but different strike prices.

volatility The size and rate at which price moves.

Index

Also in the Made Simple series

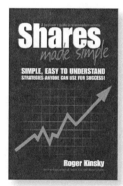  

Available from all good bookshops

Printed in Australia
08 Nov 2024
LP036873